Sports Illustrated KIDS

PRO FILES:
BASEBALL

Intel on Today's Biggest Stars
AND
Tips on How to Play Like Them

Managing Editor, Sports Illustrated Kids **Bob Der**

Project Editor **Andrea Woo**

Creative Director **Beth Bugler**

Director of Photography **Marguerite Schropp Lucarelli**

Photo Editors **Annmarie Avila, Porter Binks**

Writers **Albert Chen,
Gary Gramling, Joe Lemire**

Editors **Justin Tejada, Sachin Shenolikar**

Copy Editor **Megan Collins**

Reporter **Ryan Hatch**

Designers **Mary Mathieux, Kirsten Sorton**

Imaging **Geoffrey Michaud,
Dan Larkin, Robert Thompson**

Special thanks to: Myles Ringel, Jeffrey Kaji,
Georgia Millman-Perlah, Alex Borinstein,
Peyton Frazier, Jarret Harrison

TIME HOME ENTERTAINMENT

Publisher **Richard Fraiman**
Vice President, Business Development & Strategy **Steven Sandonato**
Executive Director, Marketing Services **Carol Pittard**
Executive Director, Retail & Special Sales **Tom Mifsud**
Executive Director, New Product Development **Peter Harper**
Editorial Director **Stephen Koepp**
Director, Bookazine Development & Marketing **Laura Adam**
Publishing Director **Joy Butts**
Finance Director **Glenn Buonocore**
Assistant General Counsel **Helen Wan**
Assistant Director, Special Sales **Ilene Schreider**
Design & Prepress Manager **Anne-Michelle Gallero**
Book Production Manager **Susan Chodakiewicz**
Brand Manager **Allison Parker**
Associate Prepress Manager **Alex Voznesenskiy**
Special thanks: Christine Austin, Jeremy Biloon, Jim Childs, Rose Cirrincione,
Jacqueline Fitzgerald, Christine Font, Jenna Goldberg, Lauren Hall, Carrie Hertan,
Hillary Hirsch, Suzanne Janso, Amy Mangus, Robert Marasco, Kimberly Marshall,
Amy Migliaccio, Nina Mistry, Dave Rozzelle, Adriana Tierno, Vanessa Wu

ISBN 10: 1-60320-238-2
ISBN 13: 978-1-60320-238-1
Library of Congress Control Number: 2011940564

We welcome your comments and suggestions about Sports Illustrated Kids Books.
Please write to us at:
Sports Illustrated Kids Books, Attention: Book Editors, P.O. Box 11016,
Des Moines, IA 50336-1016. If you would like to order any of our hardcover
Collector's Edition books, please call us at 1-800-327-6388, Monday through
Friday, 7 a.m. to 8 p.m., or Saturday, 7 a.m. to 6 p.m., Central Time.

1 QGV 11

JUSTIN VERLANDER

Detroit Tigers pitcher,
2011 American League Cy Young Award
winner and MVP

CONTENTS

Dustin Pedroia
Team: Boston Red Sox
Position: Second Baseman
Page 6

Justin Verlander
Team: Detroit Tigers
Position: Pitcher
Page 12

Albert Pujols
Team: Los Angeles Angels
Position: First Baseman
Page 18

Joe Mauer
Team: Minnesota Twins
Position: Catcher
Page 24

Justin Upton
Team: Arizona Diamondbacks
Position: Rightfielder
Page 30

Evan Longoria
Team: Tampa Bay Rays
Position: Third Baseman
Page 36

Roy Halladay
Team: Philadelphia Phillies
Position: Pitcher
Page 42

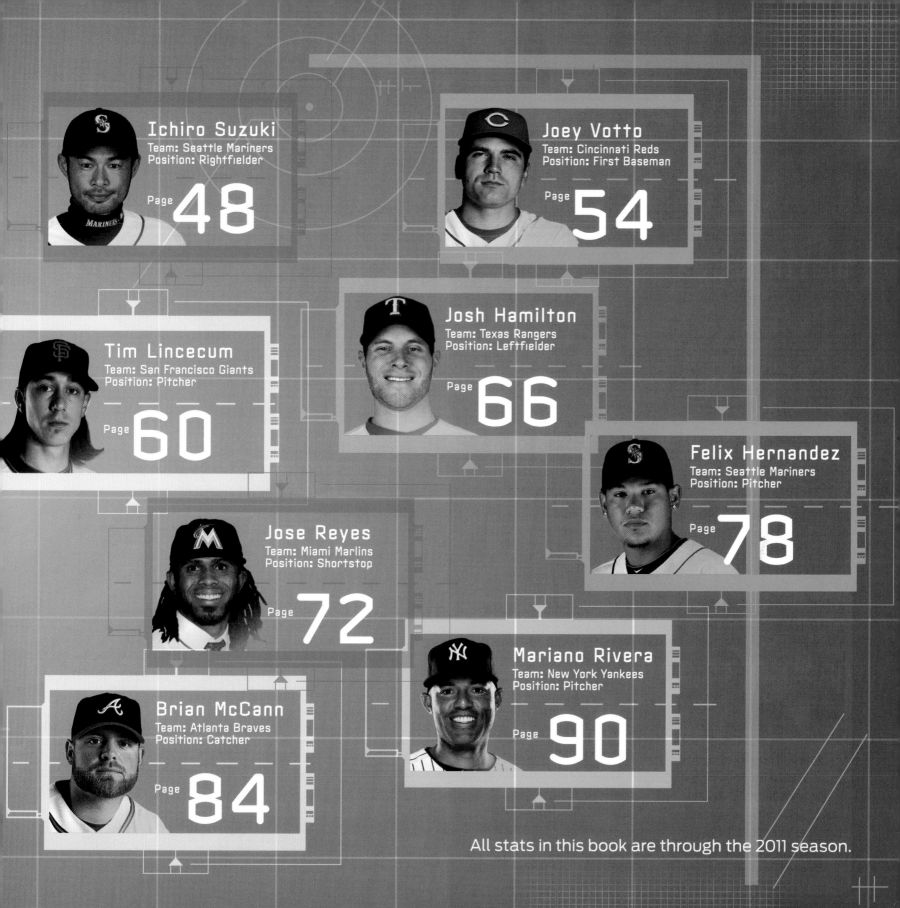

Ichiro Suzuki
Team: Seattle Mariners
Position: Rightfielder
Page 48

Joey Votto
Team: Cincinnati Reds
Position: First Baseman
Page 54

Tim Lincecum
Team: San Francisco Giants
Position: Pitcher
Page 60

Josh Hamilton
Team: Texas Rangers
Position: Leftfielder
Page 66

Felix Hernandez
Team: Seattle Mariners
Position: Pitcher
Page 78

Jose Reyes
Team: Miami Marlins
Position: Shortstop
Page 72

Mariano Rivera
Team: New York Yankees
Position: Pitcher
Page 90

Brian McCann
Team: Atlanta Braves
Position: Catcher
Page 84

All stats in this book are through the 2011 season.

PRO FILE:

DUSTIN

PEDROI

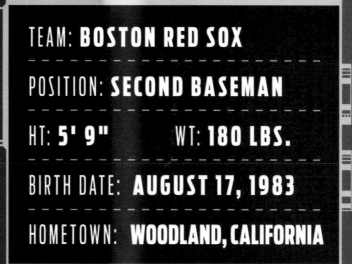

TEAM: **BOSTON RED SOX**

POSITION: **SECOND BASEMAN**

HT: **5' 9"**   WT: **180 LBS.**

BIRTH DATE: **AUGUST 17, 1983**

HOMETOWN: **WOODLAND, CALIFORNIA**

A

310

DUSTIN PEDROIA

>> Boston Red Sox second baseman Dustin Pedroia may be slight in stature (the Red Sox list him at 5'9", which is probably two inches too generous), but his list of accomplishments is long: college All-America, American League Rookie of the Year, AL MVP, and World Series champion. Pedroia has proven just how unimportant size can be. Even as a high school sophomore who weighed only 120 pounds, he was the starting varsity shortstop at Woodland (California) High. He was so good in high school that he had his pick of college scholarships and chose to play at Arizona State, one of the country's top baseball programs.

Pedroia started all 185 games of his college career and batted .384 while winning two national defensive player of the year awards. Still, after the Red Sox used their top pick to select him in the 2004 draft, a minor league manager called the front office to make sure he had received the right player, because Pedroia was so small. Players of that size are thought to be good only when they can outwork and out-hustle opponents, but Pedroia proved he can do more than that.

BOSTON'S BEST
After winning the World Series with the Red Sox in 2007, Pedroia won the American League MVP award in 2008.

"*Scrappy* is the word he can't get away from," Chicago Cubs president Theo Epstein says. "It's [lousy] because it undersells him. [It says] that all he's doing is outworking people. He's a great baseball player."

>>Immediate Impact

Pedroia made his major league debut in 2006, five days after his 23rd birthday, and won the AL Rookie of the Year in 2007 after batting .317. In the playoffs that season, he hit two home runs and scored 12 runs to help Boston win the World Series.

In 2008, Pedroia was even better, batting .326 while leading the majors in hits (213) and doubles (54), and ranking first in the AL in runs (118). He won the MVP and a Gold Glove for his defense. Pedroia doesn't take any of those achievements for granted. "I never thought that [so much] would happen at the early part of my career, [but] I'm going to keep working as hard as I can to become a better player," he says.

When Pedroia hits a hard line drive, the ball looks like a laser coming off his bat, which earned him the nickname Laser Show. Confident, outgoing, and quick to make a joke, he often suggests that opponents wear sunglasses because of the lasers they'll see at night. But he's more than just a big personality. He works hard at improving his game and is often the first player to arrive at the ballpark each day. Despite batting just .181 in the first 127 at-bats of his major league career, Pedroia was determined to get better, and he's batted .306 ever since. In 2011 he had his first 20–20 season with 21 homers and 26 stolen bases.

As Boston's designated hitter David Ortiz says, "I don't think there was a player born before him and I don't think there will be a player born after him that cares about baseball more than Dustin Pedroia."

COLLEGE
Arizona State (2002–04)

MINOR LEAGUE TEAMS
Augusta, Sarasota, Portland, Pawtucket (2004–06)

MAJOR LEAGUE TEAM
Boston Red Sox (2006–present)

CAREER STATS

GP	AVG	HR	RBI
715	.305	75	344

RUNNING THE NUMBERS

213

Hits by Pedroia during his MVP season in 2008, which led the majors. He also led the majors with 54 doubles and was tops in the AL with 118 runs scored.

5

Rookies of the Year who also won a league MVP trophy in one of their first two major league seasons: Pedroia, Ryan Howard, Ichiro, Cal Ripken Jr., and Fred Lynn.

2

Gold Gloves won by Pedroia for his defense at second base.

INSIDE INFORMATION

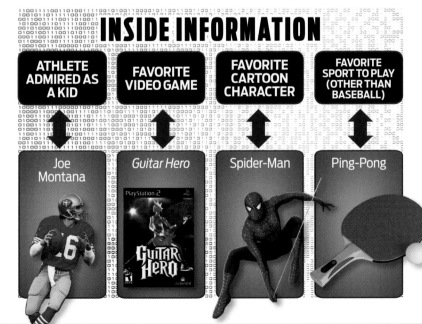

ATHLETE ADMIRED AS A KID	FAVORITE VIDEO GAME	FAVORITE CARTOON CHARACTER	FAVORITE SPORT TO PLAY (OTHER THAN BASEBALL)
Joe Montana	Guitar Hero	Spider-Man	Ping-Pong

SECRETS TO HIS GAME

Turn a Double Play Like Dustin Pedroia

Turning a double play often looks glamorous, with shortstops and second basemen rapidly catching the ball and firing to first, while jumping to avoid the runner sliding hard into the base. But learning that skill is hard work. There's a lot to consider. "At this level, with the speed of the game, how the ball is hit, how hard, and where the throw is dictates if I go across the base or stay behind it," says Pedroia. But Pedroia urges young players not to overthink the job. "You've got to simplify it into two steps," he says. "Just make sure you catch it first and throw it second." Everything else builds off that.

KNOW THE DRILL

The catch-and-throw objectives of turning a double play are easier to execute if you know how to use your feet well. "I used to draw a circle around the base and made sure that my feet always stayed inside the circle," Pedroia says. "If my feet move short [distances], I'm always going to be quick, and my shoulder's going to square up to first base, so I just try to stay inside that circle. I want to keep my footwork inside this close area, so I can catch, and then turn and throw." With practice, a player can become more precise and do the drill with circles that get smaller and smaller. "The shorter you go, the better your footwork has to be," Pedroia says.

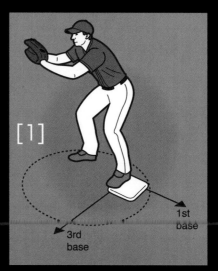

[1]

3rd base

1st base

[2]

In each at-bat, Pedroia may look like he's trying to swing from his heels and hit a home run, but in reality his maximum-effort hack is very effective at making contact and hitting line drives. Pedroia has batted as high as .326 in a season, and from 2006 through '10 he struck out only once every 11.9 plate appearances, making him the third most difficult player to strike out in the AL. That skill is particularly helpful near the top of the lineup, allowing him to advance the leadoff hitter around the bases and set the table for the heart of the order. "I think he's the best two-hole hitter in the game," former Red Sox manager Terry Francona says.

Pedroia is the rare player who continues to get faster as he gets older. He has stolen 20 or more bases three times, including a career-best 26 in 2011. His abilities to get on base and to run (with the aid of the great hitters after him in the order, of course) helped him score 474 runs in the past five seasons, the fourth most among AL players.

"He's their igniter," says a scout from an opposing team. "He's involved in all their rallies."

And he'll help stop opposing rallies too. Pedroia is an excellent fielder who has great range, snaring ground balls up the middle or toward the first-base hole.

[3]

IN HIS WORDS

" I try not to think about [my size]. I try to play the game like everyone else. Size doesn't matter. The only size that matters is [the size of] your heart."

PRO F

VER

TEAM: **DETROIT TIGERS**

POSITION: **PITCHER**

HT: **6' 5"**   WT: **225 LBS.**

BIRTH DATE: **FEBRUARY 20, 1983**

HOMETOWN: **GOOCHLAND, VIRGINIA**

CLE:

JUSTIN
RLANDER

PRO FILES: BASEBALL

15

JUSTIN VERLANDER

BACKGROUND REPORT

>> When Justin Verlander was 10 years old, he and his father were skipping stones across a small pond near their home in Goochland County, Virginia. His father, Richard, picked a rock and threw it as far as he could, his toss plopping halfway across the pond. Then Justin grabbed his own rock and chucked it across the entire pond. "At that moment, I was like, 'This kid has got a special arm,'" Richard remembers.

Verlander, the 6'5" ace of the Detroit Tigers, has always had a natural ability to throw hard and far, but he has worked at his craft, too. To practice long toss, Verlander would drag his family to a local football field, where his mother, father, and brother would relay his 100-yard throws back to him. When Verlander was in high school, his father hired a former college pitching coach, Bob Smith, to teach his son. From Smith, Verlander learned how to pitch to hitters, not just throw to the plate. "There should be purpose and knowledge behind every pitch that I throw," Verlander says. "The wrong pitch with conviction is better than the right pitch without it."

>>Rapid Rise

Verlander came into his own while attending college at Old Dominion, and the Tigers made him the Number 2 overall pick of the 2004 draft. Verlander's career began so smoothly that making further adjustments didn't immediately seem necessary. He was named 2006 Rookie of the Year, helping the Tigers win the American League pennant before losing to the St. Louis Cardinals in the World Series. In 2007 he threw his first of two career no-hitters and made the first of four All-Star teams. But he suffered a setback in 2008, losing 17 games, the most in the majors, while managing only a 4.84 ERA. Verlander quickly realized the importance of staying sharp and not growing complacent.

"For two years this game came pretty easy to me at the big-league

CAN'T BEAT THE HEAT Verlander won the 2011 American League Cy Young Award after leading the league in wins, ERA, and strikeouts.

level," Verlander says. "I'd just go out there, throw, and things fell into place for me. I'm not saying it is an easy game. I quickly found out that it's not. It just seemed that this was the way it was going to be forever. I guess, maybe, through that process I lost a little bit of my edge."

>>A Season to Remember

Early in the 2009 season, Verlander committed himself to being mentally strong by cutting out all distractions before he pitches and keeping his focus sharp during games. This approach led to his historic 2011 season: Verlander was unanimously named the AL Cy Young Award winner after completing the pitching Triple Crown by leading the league in wins (24), ERA (2.40), and strikeouts (250). A few days later, he was named the AL MVP, becoming the first pitcher to win the award since Dennis Eckersley of the Oakland A's in 1992 and the first starter since the Boston Red Sox's Roger Clemens in 1986.

Verlander's fastball is so fast and his curveball breaks so much that he struck out an average of one batter per inning while walking the fewest batters of his career (only two for every nine innings he pitched). His intelligence, his cannon arm, and his durability (he's thrown five straight seasons of 200 or more innings) are the reasons why Verlander is one of baseball's elite pitchers.

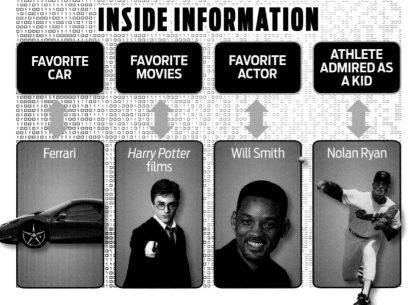

INSIDE INFORMATION

FAVORITE CAR	FAVORITE MOVIES	FAVORITE ACTOR	ATHLETE ADMIRED AS A KID
Ferrari	*Harry Potter* films	Will Smith	Nolan Ryan

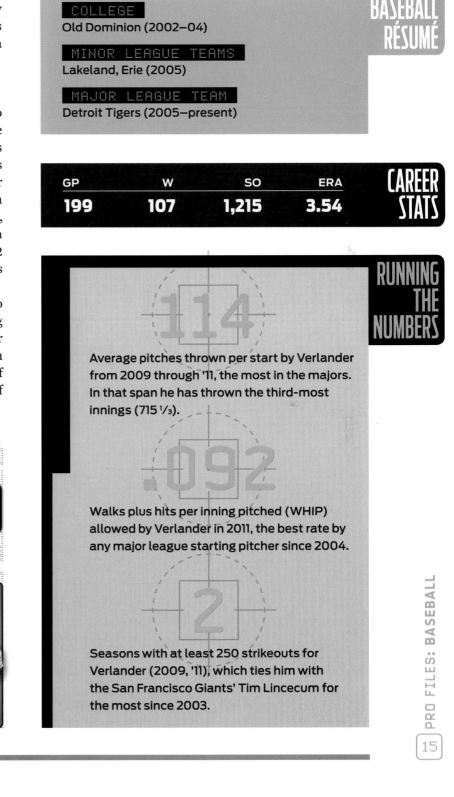

COLLEGE
Old Dominion (2002–04)

MINOR LEAGUE TEAMS
Lakeland, Erie (2005)

MAJOR LEAGUE TEAM
Detroit Tigers (2005–present)

CAREER STATS

GP	W	SO	ERA
199	107	1,215	3.54

RUNNING THE NUMBERS

114

Average pitches thrown per start by Verlander from 2009 through '11, the most in the majors. In that span he has thrown the third-most innings (715 1/3).

.092

Walks plus hits per inning pitched (WHIP) allowed by Verlander in 2011, the best rate by any major league starting pitcher since 2004.

2

Seasons with at least 250 strikeouts for Verlander (2009, '11), which ties him with the San Francisco Giants' Tim Lincecum for the most since 2003.

SECRETS TO HIS GAME

Command Your Pitches Like Justin Verlander

Even the best pitchers struggle with control, and Verlander was forced to learn how to harness his pitches at an early age. As a teen, he was already a hard thrower — his AAU catcher, Mike Vranian, wore quarter-inch padded gloves under his mitt to avoid bruising — but Verlander wasn't the most accurate pitcher. Says Vranian, "The first batter would either walk, because Justin was so wild, or he'd strike out, out of fear."

Eventually Verlander's AAU coach Bob Smith implemented a rule that Verlander had to throw two simulated innings in the bullpen before taking the mound, in order to get him to settle down. Smith finally harnessed the erratic arm by forcing him into situations with little margin for error. A 15-year-old Verlander was made the closer for an elite 18-and-under fall showcase. "When a kid's backed in a corner, sometimes they react in a positive way," Smith says.

For his first save opportunity, Verlander entered in the bottom of the ninth with a 1–0 lead. His first 12 pitches — all fastballs — missed the strike zone, and he loaded the bases on three walks. Smith called time and jogged to the mound. "What are you doing?" he barked at Verlander, who responded, "I don't know." Smith chewed him out, saying he should never give "I don't know" as an answer. The coach then instructed him to throw only curves — and Verlander struck out the next three guys on 11 breaking balls, missing the strike zone only twice. Said Smith, "It was a defining moment for him."

IN HIS WORDS

" It's hard for me to put a finger on what I know, but it's there. Time. Experience of pitching at this level for a while now. You log it all away, and it opens up a new game to you."

THE REPEATABLE DELIVERY

Verlander has never had to make major changes to his delivery, but over the years he's made tweaks. He's now mastered what's called a repeatable delivery. That means he's comfortable enough with his delivery that he can repeat it over and over again without having to think about it. His mechanics are simple and fluid, with his whole body working in sync with his arm. That repeatable delivery has led to better control. It also means less stress on his arm. Through six seasons, Verlander had never spent a day on the disabled list. And while most pitchers wear down as the game goes on, Verlander's velocity is still there late in games. During a no-hitter in Toronto in 2011, he threw a 100 mile-per-hour fastball to the last batter of the game.

PLAYER ANALYSIS

[+] Verlander has a powerful
[+] right arm, capable of
[+] throwing fastballs in excess
[+] of 100 miles per hour. But he's
[+] most effective when he's
[+] painting the corners, which
[+] makes his pitches extra
[+] difficult to hit. "He throws
[+] strikes," Rangers manager
[+] Ron Washington says. "He
[+] goes out of the strike zone by
[+] design. So when he's in the
[+] strike zone and he gives you a
[+] pitch to hit — this is easy to

[+] say, but it's not easy to do —
[+] don't miss it. Try not to
[+] chase."
[+] A common strategy for
[+] hitters facing great pitchers is
[+] to be patient at the plate. The
[+] idea is that the more a pitcher
[+] throws, the more tired he gets
[+] and the easier it will be to get
[+] a hit. But that doesn't work
[+] against Verlander, who has
[+] averaged the most pitches per
[+] start of all major leaguers in
[+] each of the last three seasons.

[+] "You don't have to worry
[+] about building up his pitch
[+] count, because the pitch
[+] count with this guy just goes
[+] out the door," says
[+] Washington.
[+] Verlander has been known
[+] to hit 100 miles per hour or
[+] faster even when his pitch
[+] count is at 100 pitches or
[+] higher. "With Verlander, you
[+] feel lucky any time you get a
[+] hit," says longtime big leaguer
[+] Orlando Cabrera.

PRO FILE:

ALBERT

TEAM: **LOS ANGELES ANGELS**

POSITION: **FIRST BASEMAN**

HT: **6' 3"**   WT: **230 LBS.**

BIRTH DATE: **JANUARY 16, 1980**

HOMETOWN: **SANTO DOMINGO,
DOMINICAN REPUBLIC**

PUJOLS

ALBERT PUJOLS

BACKGROUND REPORT

>> As one of the greatest sluggers of his generation, Albert Pujols has hit many home runs that have reached legendary — and almost mythical — status. There was the

home run he hit as a senior at Liberty (Missouri) High, a drive that sailed over the 402-foot fence in centerfield and crashed into an air-conditioning unit atop a two-story building. There was the moon shot he launched as a college sophomore over the leftfield wall of Highland (Kansas) Community College, which soared across a street and over a tree. There was the game-winning three-run dinger in the ninth inning in Game 5 of the 2005 NL Championship Series that landed over the train tracks beyond leftfield at Houston's Minute Maid Park. And there was his ninth-inning blast on the night he had the greatest offensive game in World Series history, a missile to leftfield at Rangers Ballpark in Game 3 of the 2011 Fall Classic that made him only the third player in history to hit three home runs in a World Series game.

>>All-Time Great

Asking Pujols to pick the greatest and most memorable home run of his career is a little like asking Michelangelo to choose his favorite work of art. "I've been fortunate to have so many amazing moments in my career, it's hard to choose one home run that's more special than another," says Pujols. "When my career is over, maybe then I'll be able to look back, and maybe then, one will stand out."

When that time comes, Pujols will undoubtedly be reflecting on one of the greatest careers in major league history. Few players have accomplished what Pujols has in 11 seasons: 10 All-Star selections, three National League MVP awards, and two World Series rings. "He's a player that you'll tell your grandkids you played with," says Cardinals rightfielder Lance Berkman. "It's a privilege to be able to watch him play."

CONTACT SPORT
A three-time NL MVP, Pujols had the highest career batting average (.329) among active players through 2011.

>>Straight to the Top

Baseball has always been in Pujols's blood. His father, Bienvenido, was an accomplished softball pitcher in the Dominican Republic. As a boy in

Santo Domingo, little Albert would proudly wear his father's jersey around the neighborhood. He lived the typical life of a Dominican boy, playing baseball on scraggly fields in his neighborhood.

Pujols, who moved to Missouri with his father when he was 16, was an accomplished high school player in Independence, Missouri, and at Maple Woods Community College in Kansas City. But he wasn't drafted until the 13th round of the 1999 amateur draft, when St. Louis selected him. Pujols wasted little time in showing the teams that had passed on him that they had made a very big mistake. He jumped from A ball to Triple A in his first minor league season. The next spring, in 2001, when he was a non-roster invitee to Cardinals training camp, he played his way onto the big-league roster. After one of the greatest rookie seasons in history — he hit .329 with 37 homers and 130 RBIs — Tony La Russa, then the Cardinals manager, signed a photo he had taken with Pujols and wrote, "To Albert, The best player I've ever coached."

Ten years later, La Russa's words rang true as he and Pujols celebrated their second championship together after St. Louis defeated the Rangers in the 2011 World Series. Now La Russa was ready to heap even more praise. "Not only is he the best player I've managed, but when you talk about the great players in the history of the game, Albert's in the discussion," he said. The victory marked an end to Pujols's career in St. Louis. About a month later, he signed a contract to play for the Los Angeles Angels. "I'm going to try to bring what I have learned in the city of St. Louis here," said Pujols. "I'm just really excited to go out there and do my best, like I did in St. Louis for 11 years."

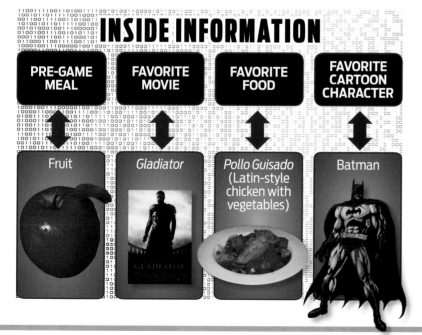

INSIDE INFORMATION

PRE-GAME MEAL	FAVORITE MOVIE	FAVORITE FOOD	FAVORITE CARTOON CHARACTER
Fruit	Gladiator	Pollo Guisado (Latin-style chicken with vegetables)	Batman

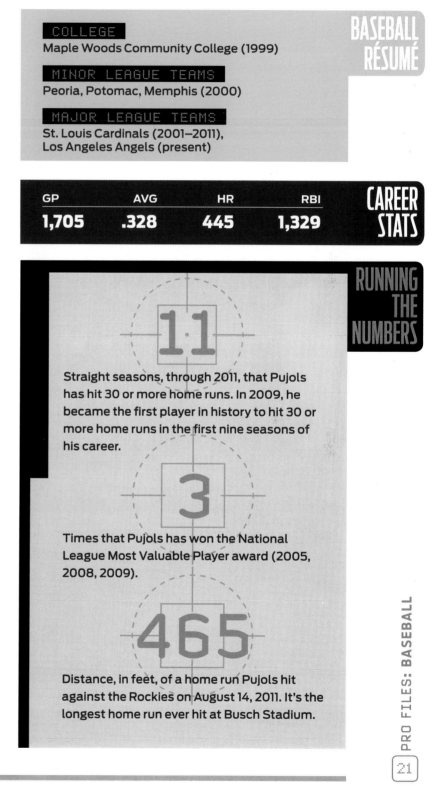

RUNNING THE NUMBERS

11
Straight seasons, through 2011, that Pujols has hit 30 or more home runs. In 2009, he became the first player in history to hit 30 or more home runs in the first nine seasons of his career.

3
Times that Pujols has won the National League Most Valuable Player award (2005, 2008, 2009).

465
Distance, in feet, of a home run Pujols hit against the Rockies on August 14, 2011. It's the longest home run ever hit at Busch Stadium.

SECRETS TO HIS GAME

Stand at the Plate Like Albert Pujols

Pujols holds his hands level with his right ear and bounces his right elbow three or four times to keep his hands relaxed. "If you're too stiff, then your hands can't be that quick," says Pujols.

Pujols does not take a big step with his front foot when he swings. Instead, he drives forward with his hips.

When Pujols steps up to the plate, he settles into his batting stance with his feet spread wide apart and with about 60 percent of his weight on his back foot.

POWER SURGE

Coaches say that the key to Pujols's swing is his hand speed. Because he can react faster than a lot of hitters, Pujols sees the ball for a longer period of time before he swings. And when he connects, he has the muscles to drill the ball — like he did here during Game 3 of the 2011 World Series — thanks to weightlifting that strengthens his forearms and wrists. "His hand strength is incredible," says Cardinals rightfielder Lance Berkman.

MIND GAME

You may not be able to duplicate Pujols's strength, but you can copy his approach to the game. "This game is mental more than physical," says Cardinals hitting coach Mark McGwire. "Number 5 is probably the strongest mental person I've ever been around. He's also the most prepared." Pujols studies videos of pitchers like they are math problems. After each game, he goes to a video room to review his swing to make sure that his approach remains consistent. That thorough understanding of the game allows Pujols to make the most of each plate appearance. "I can count on one hand the number of at-bats I've seen him give away," says McGwire.

My strength is that I'm a smart player. If someone tells me to do something, I change it quickly. If there's something wrong with my hitting, tell me what's wrong and I'll pick it up right away. That's the best thing I have — my ability to listen to a coach and fix what I'm doing wrong."

PLAYER ANALYSIS

[+] Pujols's swing is a thing of
[+] beauty. It is a simple but
[+] flawless stroke that
[+] generates staggering power.
[+] "He's able to repeat it over
[+] and over," says Berkman.
[+] Pujols covers the whole plate
[+] and often drives the ball even
[+] harder to the opposite field
[+] than he does when he's
[+] pulling the ball.
[+]   Pujols uses different bats
[+] depending on if he's facing
[+] lefthanded or righthanded
[+] pitchers. Against lefties, he
[+] swings a 33-ounce bat. When
[+] he's up against a righty,
[+] Pujols uses a bat that's one
[+] ounce lighter in order to keep
[+] him from trying to pull the
[+] ball. As a result, he rarely

[+] strikes out.
[+] "Lefthander,
[+] righthander, soft
[+] thrower, power guy,
[+] fastballs away,
[+] fastballs in — he
[+] doesn't have any
[+] holes," says McGwire.
[+]   But Pujols's
[+] greatness goes
[+] beyond what he does at the
[+] plate. After switching from
[+] outfield to first base in 2004,
[+] he evolved into one of the top
[+] fielders in the game, winning
[+] a Gold Glove in 2006 and
[+] 2010. "People overlook his
[+] defense," says former
[+] Cardinals manager Tony
[+] La Russa, "but he's the
[+] whole package."

PRO FILE: JOE MAUER

TEAM: **MINNESOTA TWINS**

POSITION: **CATCHER**

HT: **6' 5"**   WT: **235 LBS.**

BIRTH DATE: **APRIL 19, 1983**

HOMETOWN: **ST. PAUL, MINNESOTA**

BACKGROUND REPORT

>> When he was in high school, Joe Mauer was in a position that many young athletes would be jealous of. He had to make the tough decision to become either one of baseball's top prospects or college football's next great quarterback.

As a senior at Cretin-Derham Hall High School (St. Paul, Minnesota) in 2000–01, Mauer became the first athlete selected as the *USA Today* High School Player of the Year in two sports. As a quarterback, he threw for 3,022 yards and 41 touchdowns, including a state-record-tying seven TDs in the regional finals. For the baseball team, he batted .605 and hit home runs in seven consecutive games, tying a national record. He signed a letter of intent to play quarterback for Florida State, which had just won a national title. But when the hometown Minnesota Twins made him the Number 1 overall pick of the 2001 MLB draft, Mauer chose the big leagues. "[As a kid] I followed Kent Hrbek and Kirby Puckett," Mauer said of the Twins legends. "It's unbelievable to look down and see Twins [on my uniform]."

HOMETOWN LOVE
A native of St. Paul, Minnesota, Mauer chose baseball over college football when he was drafted by the Twins.

.365 batting average. He won the American League MVP award in a landslide vote.

>>Patience Pays Off

Mauer wasn't ready for the majors right away. He spent three seasons in the minors, and during that time a lot of people felt the Twins may have made a mistake by drafting him. Mauer was a promising prospect, but the Number 2 pick in his draft, Chicago Cubs pitcher Mark Prior, had already emerged as a star.

It took a few years, but Mauer proved Minnesota right. He made his big league debut on Opening Day in 2004 as a 20-year-old, getting two hits and two walks in five trips to the plate. A knee injury cut his season short, but Mauer still hit .308 with 15 extra-base hits in 35 games. Two seasons later, he won his first batting title, hitting .347 and making his first All-Star team. In 2009, Mauer added some power to his game, slugging a career-high 28 home runs to go along with a

>>Position Change?

Mauer is more than just a force at the plate, though. Playing one of the most physically demanding positions, he also takes pride in his work *behind* the plate. "I want to take care of the defense first," Mauer has said. "That's a big part of the game."

Catching has taken a toll on Mauer in recent years. In 2011, he missed 80 games with back and knee injuries, and he hit a career-low .287 when he was in the lineup. By the end of the 2011 season the Twins had started using him at first base. So what did his teammates think of Mauer's ability to gobble up ground balls? "Pretty incredible," said Carl Pavano, the starting pitcher when Mauer made his debut at first. Mauer has already gone from star QB to top-notch catcher to batting champion. Don't be surprised if he adds Gold Glove first baseman to the list.

HIGH SCHOOL
Cretin-Derham Hall

MINOR LEAGUE TEAMS
Elizabethton, Quad Cities, Fort Myers, New Britain, Rochester (2001–04)

MAJOR LEAGUE TEAM
Minnesota Twins (2004–present)

CAREER STATS

GP	AVG	HR	RBI
918	.323	84	502

RUNNING THE NUMBERS

.365

Mauer's batting average in 2009, the all-time highest single-season average by a catcher.

3

Batting titles that Mauer has won, the most ever by a catcher.

5,372,606

All-Star votes for Mauer in 2010, the fourth-most of all time.

INSIDE INFORMATION

FAVORITE VIDEO GAME	FAVORITE FOOD	FAVORITE TEAM	FAVORITE SPORT TO PLAY (OTHER THAN BASEBALL)
MLB The Show	Italian	Minnesota Vikings	Basketball

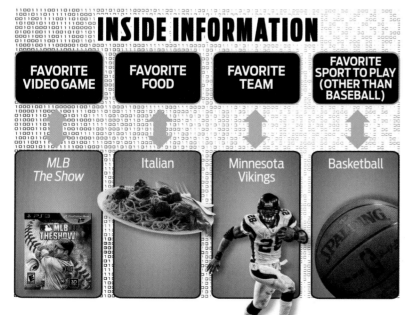

SECRETS TO HIS GAME

Throw Out a Base Runner Like Joe Mauer

Making the throw to second base can be tough for young catchers, since it's such a long distance. Even if your throw is coming up short, it's important to master the proper mechanics. If you do, when you improve your arm strength, you'll be able to get the ball to second base as quickly as possible.

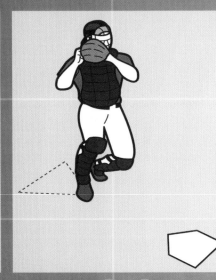

[1]

[2]

[3]

Think about making a triangle with your feet, says Terry Steinbach, a former All-Star catcher who works with Twins backstops during spring training. When you're crouching down, your two feet should form the base of the triangle.

When you come out of your crouch, the first step (for righthanded throwers) should be forward with your right foot, making the third point in the triangle. Then step toward second base with your left foot and make an over-the-top throw. "I see a lot of young catchers running forward and leaning," says Steinbach. "But you want good balance when you throw."

Good throwing mechanics have to become a habit, says Steinbach. "A lot of times players get lazy and start dropping down, throwing sidearm or three quarters," he says. "But it should always be step and throw, over-the-top. I hear [Twins manager Ron Gardenhire] say it a million times during spring training: 'Step and throw, step and throw.' And he's talking to major leaguers!"

PLAYER ANALYSIS

[+] When Mauer was a kid, his [+] dad built a special device out [+] of PVC pipe that he now calls [+] the Quickswing. The ball [+] would drop out of the pipe [+] quickly, so Mauer had to act [+] fast with a short, compact [+] swing. That's a big reason he [+] can now wait on a pitch until [+] the last moment and drive it [+] anywhere on the field.

[+] Mauer has had some [+] problems hitting for power [+] the past few seasons. He's [+] had nagging injuries, and [+] the Twins' new ballpark, [+] Target Field, is one of the [+] toughest hitter's parks in [+] baseball. But the potential [+] is still there.

[+] "When he's healthy, he's a [+] 25-home run, 100-RBI guy,"

[+] says an AL scout. "In recent [+] years, there were balls that [+] normally he would crush that [+] instead he fouled off. But he [+] shouldn't get anything less [+] than 20 home runs and [+] 80 RBIs [in a season]."

[+] Mauer is also a top [+] defensive catcher. Despite [+] being big for his position [+] (6' 5"), he's quick getting out [+] of his crouch to track down [+] bunts or throw out base [+] runners. In 2007, he showed [+] off the arm that made him a

[+] star quarterback, throwing [+] out 53.3 percent of base [+] stealers. "He's unbelievably [+] accurate [as a thrower]," says [+] the scout. "He would just [+] catch it, get rid of it, and it [+] was right there on target."

KNOW THE DRILL

Many young catchers have a bad habit of coming out of their crouch before they move to block a pitch in the dirt. To practice blocking, have a coach or teammate stand behind you and ask the pitcher to throw pitches intentionally in the dirt. As the pitch is coming in, the coach should gently push the catcher in the lower back, down and toward the pitch. When practicing, use a tennis ball rather than a hardball. "Blocking a baseball with your wrist or forearm can hurt," says Steinbach, "but you have to learn not to be afraid of the ball."

" Although catching might beat you up a little bit physically and mentally, I love the demands that are put on me and the responsibilities that I have."

PRO FILE:

JUSTIN UPTON

JUSTIN UPTON

BACKGROUND REPORT

>> Growing up in Norfolk, Virginia, brothers Justin and B.J. Upton pitched tennis balls to each other in one-on-one baseball games in their front yard. B.J. was three years older, which meant that the games often ended with Justin quitting in frustration and running into the house. "B.J. never took it easy on him," says their dad, Manny, who played college baseball at Norfolk State.

Justin soon learned that the best way to keep up was to work hard and stay confident. "The older we got, and the better I got, the longer the games went," Justin says. "I hated losing when I was younger, and I still hate losing now." But he says of his brother, who's now an outfielder for the Tampa Bay Rays, "I wouldn't have wanted B.J. to let me win."

Justin always loved to compete, especially with B.J.'s friends and teammates, all of whom were bigger and stronger. Three of those players from the same area of Virginia became major league third basemen: David Wright of the New York Mets, Ryan Zimmerman of the Washington Nationals, and Mark Reynolds of the Baltimore Orioles. Justin would tag along to their practices and participate in some drills as if he were on the team too. And it wasn't good enough just to be in their company — Justin wanted to be "as good as them right then," he says. He sometimes was. Says Wright, "You could tell

RACING AHEAD

The Number 1 pick of the 2005 draft, Upton had career-highs in hits (171), doubles (39), and stolen bases (21) in 2011.

early on that he had a lot more physical tools than a lot of the guys that were our age."

>>Great Expectations

As Upton got older, he stayed ahead of the curve. As a freshman at Hickory High, Upton was the varsity team's starting shortstop. (He didn't become a full-time outfielder until the minor leagues.) He later transferred to and starred at Great Bridge High, in part

to play for coach Wiley Lee, a former minor league ballplayer. As a senior, Upton was named the AFLAC national high school player of the year, and Arizona selected him Number 1 in the 2005 draft. Three years earlier, Tampa Bay had taken B.J. with the Number 2 overall pick, making the Uptons the first brothers to be drafted so highly.

After just two years in the minors, Justin made his major league debut at the age of 19. He was an All-Star by the time he was 21, batting .300 with 26 home runs, 86 RBIs, and 20 stolen bases in 2009. "He always had the ability," says Reynolds, formerly Upton's teammate on the Diamondbacks. "It was just a matter of him learning that he could do it up here [in the majors]."

In 2011, Upton had career highs in hits (171), doubles (39), home runs (31), RBIs (88), stolen bases (21), and on-base percentage (.369) as he made his second NL All-Star team. He also stayed healthy and played 159 games — his first season with more than 138 — in leading the Diamondbacks to their second NL West title in five seasons.

Upton has come a long way since those days in the front yard with his brother. Even though he's led Arizona to success and has lived up to the hype of being a top draft pick, Upton isn't slowing down anytime soon. Says former Arizona bench coach Bo Porter, "The standards other people might put on him aren't as high as the standards he puts on himself."

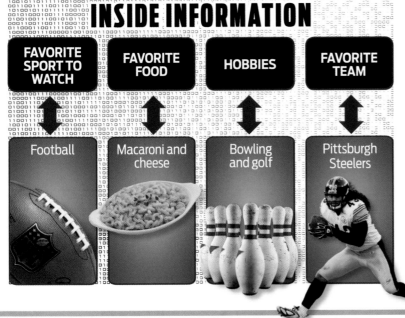

INSIDE INFORMATION

FAVORITE SPORT TO WATCH	FAVORITE FOOD	HOBBIES	FAVORITE TEAM
Football	Macaroni and cheese	Bowling and golf	Pittsburgh Steelers

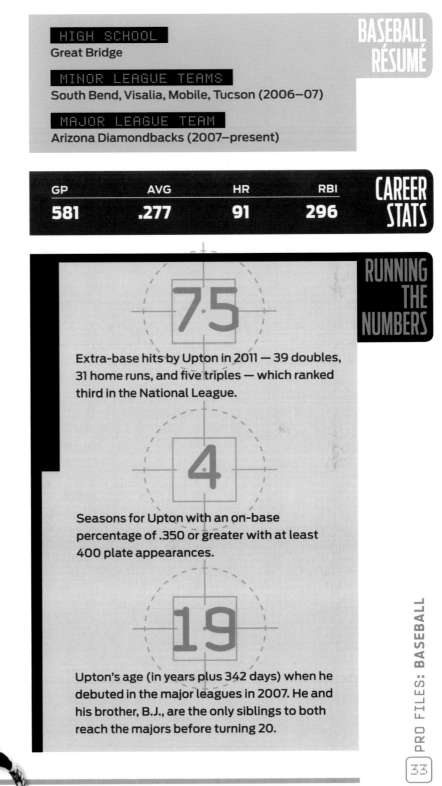

BASEBALL RÉSUMÉ

HIGH SCHOOL
Great Bridge

MINOR LEAGUE TEAMS
South Bend, Visalia, Mobile, Tucson (2006–07)

MAJOR LEAGUE TEAM
Arizona Diamondbacks (2007–present)

CAREER STATS

GP	AVG	HR	RBI
581	.277	91	296

RUNNING THE NUMBERS

7.5
Extra-base hits by Upton in 2011 — 39 doubles, 31 home runs, and five triples — which ranked third in the National League.

4
Seasons for Upton with an on-base percentage of .350 or greater with at least 400 plate appearances.

19
Upton's age (in years plus 342 days) when he debuted in the major leagues in 2007. He and his brother, B.J., are the only siblings to both reach the majors before turning 20.

SECRETS TO HIS GAME

Be an All-Around Player Like Justin Upton

The secret to becoming a great all-around player is simple: Don't overlook any aspect of your game, and focus on doing all the little things correctly. Upton is one of the game's best talents because he was committed to working hard at all his skills — not only his hitting — from a young age. To instill a proper work ethic in Upton, his high school coach Wiley Lee gave him additional work every day, including swinging off the tee, live batting practice, fielding drills, and baserunning exercises.

"Each day he had something extra he had to work on, so he understood the importance of being a well-rounded player," says Lee. "Physically he could probably dominate the majority of the high school players he faced, but we knew either an elite college or the pros would be waiting for him in the near future."

" There's a lot that goes into baseball. You have your good times and you have your bad times. That's just the way the game goes. I've been able to stay positive, and see the ball and hit the ball."

PLAYING WITH THE BIG KIDS

Upton was lucky to grow up with an older brother who, along with several of his friends, was a hot baseball prospect. Not only did Upton get to play with them — which showed him that he could keep up with stronger players — but it also got him used to seeing and performing for major league scouts.

Upton first participated in the Area Code Games, a showcase for the best high school players in the nation, as a 14-year-old. Even though he was one of the youngest players there, he was not intimidated. In one game, Upton crushed a ball to the wall of the stadium. "I took him out there just so he could get his feet wet and see how he'd compete against older guys," his father, Manny, says. "What happened was he actually surprised me."

His performance didn't go unnoticed. "He was a 14-year-old kid at the Area Code Games, and he stood out," said Washington Nationals general manager and former Diamondbacks scouting director Mike Rizzo.

PLAYER ANALYSIS

[+] The greatest discovery for any scout is the five-tool player: an athlete who excels at running, throwing, fielding, hitting for average, and hitting for power. What's scary is that Upton is a five-tool player who has yet to reach his peak.

In his first four seasons Upton has batted as high as .300, hit as many as 31 home runs, stolen as many as 21 bases, and has grown into a highly rated defensive rightfielder, despite having played mostly shortstop before he was drafted. According to an advanced statistic called Ultimate Zone Rating, which measures how many runs a player saves for his team, Upton was the second-best defensive rightfielder in the majors from 2009 through '11.

In 2011, Upton stepped up in the area that Arizona needed most: home-run hitting. "He's gotten bigger," says a scout from an opposing team. "He knows he's being paid to hit home runs."

Though Upton is still learning patience at the plate, he improved his strikeout rate considerably from 2010 to '11.

TEAM: TAMPA BAY RAYS

POSITION: THIRD BASEMAN

HT: 6' 2"   **WT:** 210 LBS.

BIRTH DATE: OCTOBER 7, 1985

HOMETOWN: DOWNEY, CALIFORNIA

PRO FILE: **EVAN LONGORIA**

SURE-HANDED
Longoria switched from shortstop to third base while at Long Beach State and has excelled at the position ever since.

BACKGROUND REPORT

>> When Evan Longoria arrived in Tampa to make his major league debut in April 2008, it was a little bittersweet. Longoria had reached the big leagues — but he was joining one of the worst teams in baseball. The Rays had lost 60 percent of their games, averaging 97.2 losses per season. No other franchise averaged more than 97 losses per year from 1998 through 2007. The team had never come within 18 games of an American League East division title.

But by the end of the season, all that had changed. With Longoria leading the way, Tampa *won* 97 games, topped the mighty New York Yankees and Boston Red Sox for the AL East crown, and — perhaps most surprising of all — went on to play in the World Series. After that, the Rays just kept on winning, making the playoffs in two of the next three seasons.

>> Long Road to Success

Tampa has had great players during its successful run: speedy leftfielder Carl Crawford, slugging first baseman Carlos Peña, and flame-throwing lefthander David Price among them. But Longoria has been the most valuable Ray and the team's leader. A big reason why is his constant drive to improve. "I definitely think with a lot of hard work, I can be a better player than I was [the previous] year," says Longoria. "And hopefully, [I'll] continue to raise the bar every year."

It was a long climb to the top for Longoria. Even though he was an all-conference player at St. John Bosco High School in southern California, he wasn't drafted by a major league club out of high school and didn't receive any scholarship offers to play college baseball. Instead Longoria, then a slender shortstop, played his freshman year at Rio Hondo Community College in Whittier, California.

"I'd be the first to tell you that coming out of high school, even junior college, I wasn't ready," Longoria once told reporters. "I couldn't play on this stage. I was skinnier, and as I grew physically, I grew baseball-wise."

At Rio Hondo, Longoria had an all-state season that caught the eye of Long Beach State University coaches. The following year, he transferred to LBSU, a top-notch program, for his sophomore season. The 49ers already had a star shortstop, future Colorado Rockies All-Star Troy Tulowitzki, so Longoria had to move to third base. He quickly became one of the best players in the amateur ranks, playing dazzling defense at third and hitting .336 in two seasons with LBSU. The once-unknown high school player was drafted third overall by Tampa in 2006. He hit .315 with 18 home runs in only 62 minor league games later that year, then hit .299 with 26 homers in 2007, his first full season as a professional.

Going into 2008, Longoria was considered by scouts to be among the best prospects in the AL. Rays manager Joe Maddon called him "the poster child of a new beginning."

>>Reaching Stardom

When Tampa third baseman Willy Aybar went down with an injury in early 2008, Longoria got his chance in the big leagues. He hit .272 with 27 home runs and 85 RBIs and won the Rookie of the Year award that season. But the playoffs were when Longoria really started to shine. He hit six home runs in his first 11 postseason games, leading the Rays to the World Series. Even though they lost to the Phillies in five games, it was an amazing turnaround for Tampa.

Longoria went on to be an All-Star in 2009 and '10, but missed parts of 2011 due to injury. It looked like a lost season for Longoria and Tampa until September rolled around. The Rays went on a tear, winning 16 of 24 games to catch up to Boston in the AL wild card standings heading into the last day of the season. In a must-win game, Tampa trailed 7–0 against the Yankees before Longoria's three-run home run in the eighth inning helped close the gap. Then, with one out in the bottom of the 12th, he ripped a pitch over the leftfield wall to send Tampa back to the playoffs.

"It was truly astonishing," Maddon said of the home run. "But it was believable that [Longoria] would do it."

BASEBALL RÉSUMÉ

COLLEGE
Rio Hondo Community College (2004),
Long Beach State University (2005–06)

MINOR LEAGUE TEAMS
Hudson Valley, Visalia, Montgomery, Durham
(2006–08)

MAJOR LEAGUE TEAM
Tampa Bay Rays (2008–present)

CAREER STATS

GP	AVG	HR	RBI
563	.274	113	401

RUNNING THE NUMBERS

113
Career home runs hit by Longoria through 2011, the second-most among AL third basemen over the span of their first four years in the big leagues.

3
All-Star appearances for Longoria in his first three seasons. He is the only third baseman to be an All-Star in each of his first three years.

28
First-place votes, out of 28, that Longoria received in 2008 to become the AL Rookie of the Year. He was the first unanimous Rookie of the Year in either league since the St. Louis Cardinals' Albert Pujols in 2001.

INSIDE INFORMATION

ATHLETE ADMIRED AS A KID	FAVORITE MOVIE	FAVORITE FOOD	FAVORITE CARTOON CHARACTER
Michael Jordan	*The Sandlot*	Steak and potatoes	Superman

SECRETS TO HIS GAME

Play the Infield Like Evan Longoria

Mistakes in the field are often caused by poor fundamentals. Baseball's best defensive infielders know how to put themselves into a position to get to the ball and make a good throw. Longoria's natural athleticism allows him to pull off jaw-dropping plays at the hot corner, but his fundamentally sound approach plays a big role too. Here are three tips from Longoria to help you become a better infielder.

[1]

"When the pitch is being thrown, I make sure I'm in an athletic position," Longoria says. "That's different for everyone, but you should have your knees bent and your balance centered so you're ready to move laterally either way."

[2]

When a ground ball comes your way, try to take it one step at a time. You want to first get in front of the ball before thinking about the throw. "No matter what, just make sure the ball ends up in your glove," says Longoria.

[3]

Once you have the ball, then it's time to make the throw. If your momentum is taking you away from your target, be sure to set your feet. "When you're setting up to throw, there should be a straight line from your back shoulder to your front shoulder pointing toward the base," says Longoria. "You want your momentum going toward your target."

KNOW THE DRILL

Improving your infield defense often comes down to simple repetition. When he was growing up in southern California, Longoria had to be resourceful to get his fielding practice in. "I had a brick wall in my backyard, so I would throw a baseball against it to get used to fielding grounders," he says. Longoria's mom would get in on the training too, feeding him ground balls. "She would have me moving side to side, really having to reach for them," Longoria says. "She made it tough!"

PLAYER ANALYSIS

[+] Great hitters like Longoria
[+] have more than just strength.
[+] "He has tremendous balance,"
[+] says a scout from an opposing
[+] team. "He's a lot like Ryan
[+] Braun. Both of those guys hit
[+] the same way they did in
[+] college. When you [get to the
[+] pros] and don't have to make
[+] a lot of adjustments, it means
[+] you're very gifted."
[+] Longoria has the power to
[+] pull the ball over the leftfield
[+] wall, but he can also drive the
[+] ball to the opposite field. "He
[+] uses the entire field," says the
[+] scout, "and he's smart enough
[+] to know when he has a chance
[+] to take a shot at driving the
[+] ball out of the park."
[+] Longoria's natural
[+] athleticism is most obvious in
[+] the field. The two-time Gold
[+] Glove winner is arguably the
[+] best defensive third baseman
[+] in baseball, with the range to
[+] get to ground balls that would
[+] normally go through the
[+] infield for a base hit.
[+] "He's more athletic than
[+] other third basemen, without
[+] a doubt," says the scout. "He
[+] has a great first step and

[+] great anticipation, and he's
[+] always in good position. [My]
[+] grading scale for arm
[+] strength is 20 to 80, and he
[+] has a 70 arm. His throws to
[+] second base for double plays
[+] are [usually] right on
[+] the mark.
[+] "The Rays always surprise
[+] people, and he's a big part of
[+] that. He is a true star," says
[+] the scout.

IN HIS WORDS

" I take a lot of pride in my defense. People get caught up in the offensive stats, the home runs, but it's like basketball. Everyone wants to be the scorer, but the guys who play the best defense win the games."

PRO FILE:

ROY HA

TEAM: **PHILADELPHIA PHILLIES**

POSITION: **PITCHER**

HT: **6' 6"** WT: **230 LBS.**

BIRTH DATE: **MAY 14, 1977**

HOMETOWN: **ARVADA, COLORADO**

LLADAY

BACKGROUND REPORT

>> When they were looking for a new home in the Denver area more than 30 years ago, the Halladay family had a very specific request: The house had to have a basement that was at least 60 feet long. Roy Halladay Jr., a commercial airline pilot, had big plans to build a batting cage and a pitching mound for his son, Roy III. The Halladays eventually found a house in Arvada, Colorado, with a basement large enough for young Roy to throw off a mound and fire baseballs through a tire and into a mattress.

The baseball education of the Philadelphia Phillies' Roy Halladay began in that basement, but there would be many more lessons to come.

>>Study Sessions

Two books helped make Halladay one of the best pitchers in baseball. When he was 13, he read Nolan Ryan's *Pitcher's Bible* and began following the book's training programs almost obsessively. Halladay learned all about proper pitching techniques and weight-training regimens, and by the time he was a senior at Arvada West High, he was one of the most sought-after hurlers in the country. He was a tall and skinny power pitcher with an over-the-top throwing motion that unleashed devastating fastballs.

The Toronto Blue Jays drafted Halladay out of high school in the first round of the 1995 draft, and three years later, he was in the majors, pitching like a polished veteran. In only his second major league start, he was one out away from a no-hitter before giving up a home run. But Halladay would struggle over the next few seasons. In 2001 he was performing so poorly that when the Blue Jays demoted him all the way down to Class A, Halladay wondered if he should quit baseball altogether. "I had lost confidence in myself," he says. "From the age of 8 to 22, I'd never had a doubt. But I was facing adversity for the first time, and I had no idea how to turn it around."

While Halladay was at Toronto's spring training facility working

WORKHORSE
From 2007 through '11 Halladay led the league in complete games with 42.

with pitching instructors, his wife, Brandy, gave him a book called *The Mental ABC's of Pitching*, written by sports psychologist Harvey Dorfman. The book became Halladay's instructional manual, as he completely revamped his over-the-top delivery (he started throwing with a lower arm angle) and began restoring his confidence. Halladay returned to the Blue Jays, and two years later he won the American League Cy Young Award. He would win the NL award in 2010, as the ace of the Phillies. Even after more than 10 seasons in the majors — he's been named an All-Star eight times — he still reads *The Mental ABC's of Pitching* several times a season.

>>Attention to Detail

Halladay has four nasty pitches — a curveball, cutter, split-finger, and four-seam fastball — but what sets him apart from his peers is his work ethic. He's usually the first one at the ballpark before games and the last one to leave. "He's the most prepared guy," says Phillies manager Charlie Manuel. "He works harder than anybody I've ever seen."

How meticulous is Halladay? He catalogues every start, every bullpen session, every workout, and every batter he's ever faced in notebooks and in his computer. Says Halladay, "What gives me confidence going into a game is knowing that I had prepared the best I possibly could."

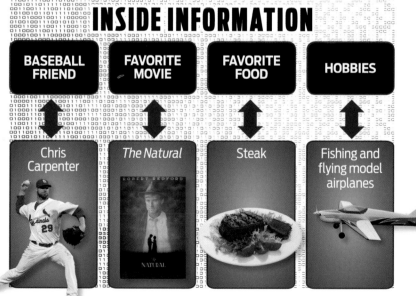

INSIDE INFORMATION

BASEBALL FRIEND	FAVORITE MOVIE	FAVORITE FOOD	HOBBIES
Chris Carpenter	*The Natural*	Steak	Fishing and flying model airplanes

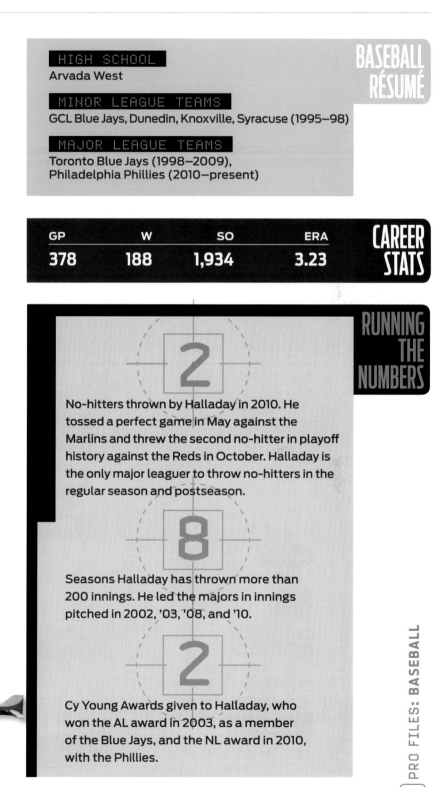

CAREER STATS

GP	W	SO	ERA
378	188	1,934	3.23

RUNNING THE NUMBERS

2
No-hitters thrown by Halladay in 2010. He tossed a perfect game in May against the Marlins and threw the second no-hitter in playoff history against the Reds in October. Halladay is the only major leaguer to throw no-hitters in the regular season and postseason.

8
Seasons Halladay has thrown more than 200 innings. He led the majors in innings pitched in 2002, '03, '08, and '10.

2
Cy Young Awards given to Halladay, who won the AL award in 2003, as a member of the Blue Jays, and the NL award in 2010, with the Phillies.

SECRETS TO HIS GAME

On Repeat

Halladay is a creature of routine. "I try to be as consistent as possible and pay close attention to detail," he says. In between starts, he lifts weights, uses an elliptical machine, runs on a treadmill, and soaks in a tub, which helps his body recover faster. On days that he starts, he won't speak to anyone before games. His pregame bullpen session is always the same: He throws 35 pitches, in five-pitch sequences broken down by different types of pitches — four-seam fastballs, cutters, change-ups, curveballs. Halladay makes sure that every pitch is thrown from the same release point. During his starts, he sits in the same spot in the dugout.

PERFECT YOUR MECHANICS LIKE ROY HALLADAY

Halladay is proof that a change in mechanics can make all the difference for a pitcher. What are the keys to a proper delivery? "Balance, direction, finish, and keeping your head on line," says A's minor league pitching coordinator Gil Patterson, who coached Halladay in the Blue Jays organization. To work those skills, Patterson recommends drawing a line in the dirt, aimed toward home plate. For righthanders, stand with the ball of your back foot on the line and the toes facing third base. (For lefties, your back foot would face first base.) As you stand, "all the weight is in the back side," says Patterson. The line represents a "tunnel that you stay in, with all the weight transferring to the front foot as you throw." The front foot should land on the line, not pointed straight at the target but turned slightly in. You don't need to throw a ball or bring up your back leg like you would when you pitch. Just practice the motion so that you get used to the way it feels. Says Patterson, "Rotating your hips and keeping your head on a line are keys."

[1]

PLANER ANALYSIS

[+] Halladay is tough to hit
[+] because of the vicious
[+] movement on his pitches.
[+] "The action on his ball is
[+] ridiculous," says Cardinals
[+] rightfielder Lance Berkman.

[+] "The ball is at your eyeballs,
[+] then before you know it, it's at
[+] your ankles." Halladay's
[+] fastball was straight until he
[+] began working on changing
[+] his delivery with Blue Jays
[+] minor league coaches,
[+] including Mel Queen and
[+] Gil Patterson. Instead of
[+] throwing the ball over the top,
[+] Halladay began throwing it
[+] from a three-quarters angle.
[+] "He started twisting his wrist
[+] a little bit, too," says
[+] Patterson, "and the way the
[+] ball started moving, it was like
[+] he was throwing a Wiffle ball."

[2]

[3]

IN HIS WORDS

"After being sent to the minors [in 2001], I told myself that if I was going to be out of baseball, I wanted to be able to look back and say I did everything to the best of my ability. I realized that I was going to have to go the extra mile from that point on. No cutting corners. The extra things are what separates people."

PRO FILE:

ICHIRO SUZUKI

TEAM: **SEATTLE MARINERS**

POSITION: **RIGHTFIELDER**

HT: **5' 11"**   WT: **170 LBS.**

BIRTH DATE: **OCTOBER 22, 1973**

HOMETOWN: **KASUGAI, JAPAN**

BACKGROUND REPORT

>> Baseball has had many all-time greats. But only a select few — Babe, Yogi — have reached such legendary status that everyone knows them by only their first name. Among today's players, Ichiro Suzuki belongs on that list. "He's Ichiro," said longtime big-league manager Dusty Baker. "That says it all, doesn't it?"

Ichiro didn't always seem destined for greatness. Growing up in Japan, he was smaller than the typical baseball star. His father trained him with a strict baseball regimen, teaching him how to both pitch and hit. While Ichiro was a natural righthanded batter, his father taught him to hit lefty in order to better take advantage of his speed.

Ichiro quickly became a local star, shining at Aikoudai Meiden High School, a top baseball program in Japan. But because of his lack of size, he wasn't drafted until the fourth and final round of Japan's Pacific League draft, by the Orix Blue Wave. His first manager, Shozo Doi, didn't think Ichiro's unorthodox swing would work in the big leagues, so Ichiro spent most of his first two pro seasons in Japan's minor leagues.

Before the 1994 season, Doi was replaced by Akira Ogi, who made Ichiro his everyday rightfielder. Ichiro rewarded his manager's confidence with a legendary season. He batted a then-league-record .385, his first of seven consecutive batting titles, and won his first of three straight MVP awards. With Ichiro leading the way, Orix won the league title the next two years.

>>MLB Debut

Ichiro dominated in Japan for seven seasons. With free agency approaching, he wanted a new challenge. After batting a career-high .387 in 2000, Ichiro became the first Japanese-born

HIT MAKER After starring in Japan for nine seasons, Ichiro came to the major leagues in 2001, and three years later broke the single-season hits record (262).

position player to make the jump to Major League Baseball. "I wanted the challenge of competing against the best players in the world," Ichiro said. "I wanted to be the first player to show what Japanese batters can do in the major leagues."

Many predicted that Ichiro would be overwhelmed by superior pitching over the longer MLB season. Instead, he hit .350, played sparkling defense, and became the second player ever to win American League MVP and Rookie of the Year in the same season. He led the Mariners to 116 wins in the regular season, the most ever by an AL team. By playoff time, teams knew how dangerous he was. "Do not let Ichiro beat you," said Joe Torre, then the Yankees manager. "He is the key to Seattle's offense."

>>Next Stop: Hall of Fame

The hits have kept on coming for Ichiro. He had at least 200 hits and batted .300 or better in each of his first 10 major league seasons. In 2004, his legend grew even larger. He broke the MLB single-season hits record with 262. He also dominated games in the field. Ichiro's speed gave him outstanding range in the outfield, and his arm was the best in baseball. An elite high school pitcher, Ichiro threw darts from rightfield to third base and home plate that not only got there fast, but got there with amazing accuracy.

Back in 2001, the question was whether a Japanese-born hitter could be an impact player in the big leagues. Ichiro's Hall of Fame career has provided the answer.

INSIDE INFORMATION

FAVORITE SUBJECT IN SCHOOL	ATHLETE ADMIRED AS A KID	HOBBY	FAVORITE VIDEO GAME
Social studies	Carl Lewis	Golf	Super Mario Bros.

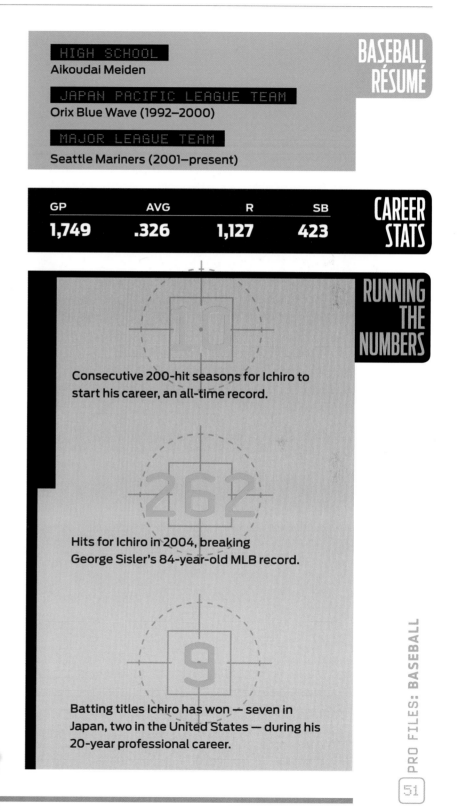

BASEBALL RÉSUMÉ

HIGH SCHOOL
Aikoudai Meiden

JAPAN PACIFIC LEAGUE TEAM
Orix Blue Wave (1992–2000)

MAJOR LEAGUE TEAM
Seattle Mariners (2001–present)

CAREER STATS

GP	AVG	R	SB
1,749	.326	1,127	423

RUNNING THE NUMBERS

10
Consecutive 200-hit seasons for Ichiro to start his career, an all-time record.

262
Hits for Ichiro in 2004, breaking George Sisler's 84-year-old MLB record.

9
Batting titles Ichiro has won — seven in Japan, two in the United States — during his 20-year professional career.

SECRETS TO HIS GAME

Throw Out Runners from the Outfield Like Ichiro

In 2010, SPORTS ILLUSTRATED polled MLB players on which outfielder had the best arm. Ichiro won with 47 percent of the vote. No one else got more than nine percent. While Ichiro's arm is strong, it's not the strongest in baseball. What really scares opposing base runners is how accurate his throws are.

When Ichiro throws from the outfield, you can see baseball fundamentals at work. His positioning and his legs are just as important as his arm. He always sets himself up so that his momentum is going toward the infield. His small "crow hop," a tiny jump off his left foot, allows him to gain his balance and transfer more power off his right foot when he throws.

As for his actual arm action, he points his glove toward his target as he gets ready to throw. That keeps his left shoulder from opening up, which would take power off his throw. As he starts to throw, his glove arm pulls down, and his throwing arm follows with an over-the-top motion.

"I'm not a big guy, and hopefully kids could look at me and see that I'm not muscular and not physically imposing. I'm just a regular guy. So if somebody with a regular body can get into the record books, kids can look at that. That would make me happy."

MASTER OF THE GAME

Ichiro is a one-of-a-kind hitter whose style is to use precise bat control to place the ball into open areas on the field. He doesn't draw a lot of walks, but that's not because he chases bad pitches. It's because he can handle any pitch, even ones out of the strike zone. Sometimes he'll slap a ball between the shortstop and third baseman. Sometimes he'll pull it over the first baseman's head.

"The game is just different for this man," Hall of Famer Paul Molitor said in 2004, when he was working with Ichiro as the Mariners hitting coach. "He sees spaces on the field and guides the ball where he wants it to go, just like he's playing slow-pitch softball."

"I wish you could put a camera at third base to see how he hits the ball and see the way it deceives you," Detroit Tigers third baseman Brandon Inge told *The New York Times*. "You can call some guys' infield hits cheap, but not his. He has amazing technique."

Considering how successful Ichiro has been, you'd think there would be more young players copying his style. "They all want to hit the ball out of the park," says an American League scout. "And some of the guys who try to play like him aren't as smart."

Will there ever be another Ichiro? "It might sound negative, but I'm not sure [there will be]," says the scout. "I don't think players can be taught to [use] the bat like Ichiro does."

PLAYER ANALYSIS

[+] Ichiro is one of the most
[+] unusual players in baseball
[+] history. He places hard-hit
[+] balls through the infield and
[+] then uses his speed on the
[+] base paths. "When he has
[+] protection in the lineup, you
[+] have to [throw strikes against
[+] him]," says an AL scout. "And
[+] when he knows he's going to
[+] get attacked, he can jump all
[+] over the ball."
[+] Pitchers don't have an easy
[+] time getting Ichiro out. "If you

[+] think you'll just throw him stuff
[+] down and away, or throw him
[+] some breaking balls, he'll hit a
[+] ball [that bounces]
[+] off the ground,"
[+] says the scout.
[+] One of Ichiro's
[+] most dangerous
[+] weapons is his
[+] speed. Since his
[+] rookie season in
[+] 2001, Ichiro has
[+] more infield hits
[+] than anyone in

[+] baseball (554), and he's
[+] third in stolen bases (423).
[+] Ichiro's speed and instincts also help him in the field. He has great range in rightfield, and in his prime, he had one of the best arms in baseball. "His arm isn't quite what it used to be, when he would make those Roberto Clemente–type throws," says the scout. "But even now, he's still very difficult to run on."

PRO FILE:

JOEY VOTTO

TEAM: **CINCINNATI REDS**

POSITION: **FIRST BASEMAN**

HT: **6' 3"** WT: **200 LBS.**

BIRTH DATE: **SEPTEMBER 10, 1983**

HOMETOWN: **TORONTO, ONTARIO, CANADA**

JOEY VOTTO

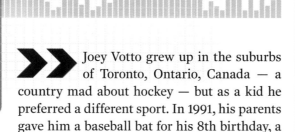

BACKGROUND REPORT

>> Joey Votto grew up in the suburbs of Toronto, Ontario, Canada — a country mad about hockey — but as a kid he preferred a different sport. In 1991, his parents gave him a baseball bat for his 8th birthday, a year before his hometown Blue Jays won the first of back-to-back World Series championships, and Votto was hooked. "I was a very big baseball fan," Votto says.

For nine or ten months of the year, Votto and his father would play catch every day after school, which was no small feat in Canada's cold climate. But Votto loved the time with his father so much that he would insist on going outside — even on holidays. "Remember this," his father told him after one outing, "because we just played catch on Christmas Day."

When his father wasn't available, Votto would walk behind the restaurant his parents owned and throw balls at a square target he had painted on the concrete wall. At the time Votto concentrated mostly on pitching, but he suffered an elbow injury when he was about 13. "I thought it was the end of the world," he says. It turned out to be a blessing in disguise. "I probably wouldn't have been a professional ballplayer if I didn't hurt my arm," Votto says. His real skill, he learned, was hitting.

>>Hitting the Mark

By high school Votto had found a group of friends who loved baseball as much as he did, so they would go hit every afternoon. "We'd hang out, and it was like our hobby," Votto says. "I don't remember watching TV or having time to play video games, but I do remember always doing baseball stuff."

That constant repetition and adherence to a practice regimen paid off. After Votto starred in high school at Richview Collegiate Institute, the Cincinnati Reds made him a second-round pick in the 2002 draft.

In September of 2007, Votto reached the big leagues and homered in the first at-bat of the first game he started. In May of the following year he hit three homers in one game against the Chicago Cubs, and he finished second in NL Rookie of the Year voting that season behind Chicago catcher Geovany Soto.

FIELDER'S CHOICE
Votto, the 2010 National League MVP, won his first Gold Glove in 2011.

>>Red Hot

Votto kept steadily improving until his game exploded in 2010. He led the National League in on-base percentage (.424) and slugging percentage (.600) while ranking in the league's top four for batting average (.324), home runs (37), RBIs (113), runs (106), and walks (91). He received 31 of 32 first-place votes to run away with the NL MVP award.

Pitchers were more careful with him in 2011. But Votto's discipline at the plate helped him lead the league with 110 walks and a .416 on-base percentage, and he still batted .309 with 29 home runs and an NL-leading 40 doubles. And, after steady off-season work to improve his fielding, he won his first Gold Glove.

Votto, still only 28 years old, is now established as one of the game's elite hitters for both power and average. His next goal is to lead the emerging Reds deep into the postseason.

HIGH SCHOOL
Richview Collegiate Institute

MINOR LEAGUE TEAMS
GCL Reds, Billings, Dayton, Potomac, Sarasota, Chattanooga, Louisville (2002–07)

MAJOR LEAGUE TEAM
Cincinnati Reds (2007–present)

CAREER STATS

GP	AVG	HR	RBI
617	.313	119	401

RUNNING THE NUMBERS

.418
On-base percentage for Votto from 2009 through '11, the best among all National League players over that time span.

31
First-place votes, out of 32, that Votto received in 2010 to win the NL MVP award. He became the first Reds player to be named MVP since Barry Larkin in 1995.

77
Years since someone had hit 10 doubles in five games before Votto accomplished the feat in September of 2009. The last player to do so was Pirates Hall of Fame outfielder Paul Waner in 1932.

INSIDE INFORMATION

FAVORITE VIDEO GAME	FAVORITE ACTOR	FAVORITE FOOD	FAVORITE SUBJECT IN SCHOOL
⬍	⬍	⬍	⬍
FIFA 11	Tom Hanks	Pizza	English

SECRETS TO HIS GAME

Hit to All Fields Like Joey Votto

Votto hit his first major-league-distance home run during batting practice at the age of 18. The lefthanded hitter smashed the ball down the rightfield line — "totally pulled," he says — and then it hit and bounced over the top of the wall. "It was like choirs started singing," he recalls. "It was such a huge moment for me. It sounds ridiculous, but little things like that mattered." The homer showed Votto his progress as a hitter. He got so serious about becoming a major leaguer that he used a wood bat in high school games. Now, the older and stronger Votto (6'3", 220 pounds) has power to all fields and he isn't focusing all his strength on yanking the ball for homers. "I can shoot a ball through the gaps now," he says. Even though he is an MVP, Votto still makes regular adjustments in his approach as he continues to establish himself. "[In 2010] I felt like every single at-bat, I had to go get it myself," Votto says. "I think you have to establish that at the beginning of your career. You have to prove [yourself] to the pitchers by being aggressive, getting a lot of extra-base hits, and doing some damage in tough spots."

GLOVE STORY

Votto admits that he used to struggle with his fielding as a young minor leaguer. "I was such a fish out of water when it came to defense when I was younger," Votto says. "I didn't know what I was doing there. I had to slow the game down." He accomplished that with lots of practice. Votto designed his own fielding drills, which he practices over and over with the help of the Reds' Double A hitting coach, Ryan Jackson, who lives near Votto in the off-season. "He's very organized," Jackson says. "You don't get where he is without being somewhat of a perfectionist. It's almost that he takes more pride in his defense." Says Votto, "Now the game is very slow, especially when I'm on defense."

PLAYER ANALYSIS

[+] A lefthanded batter, Votto
[+] knows how to hit, plain and
[+] simple. He can hit for average
[+] and for power; he can drive
[+] the ball to leftfield and pull it
[+] to rightfield. Over his last
[+] three seasons he's batted .318
[+] and averaged 30 home runs
[+] and 100 RBIs.

[+] But Votto is productive even
[+] when he doesn't swing. In 2011
[+] he led the National League by
[+] taking 110 walks and had the
[+] NL's highest on-base
[+] percentage (.416) for the
[+] second straight season. After
[+] his MVP season in 2010, pitchers
[+] were a "little more cautious" in
[+] throwing to him, he says.
[+] A big reason why Votto is so
[+] disciplined at the plate is that
[+] he is a "very studied player of
[+] this game," according to Reds
[+] rightfielder Jay Bruce. Votto
[+] watches a lot of
[+] video of opposing
[+] pitchers and
[+] constantly
[+] practices in the
[+] batting cage.
[+] And though
[+] Votto admits he
[+] wasn't
[+] comfortable
[+] playing first base
[+] early in his career, he has
[+] worked to turn that weakness
[+] into a strength. In 2011 he won
[+] his first Gold Glove. "Joey
[+] saves us," Reds manager
[+] Dusty Baker says. "All he
[+] needs to do is stay healthy
[+] and don't change anything."

IN HIS WORDS

" I felt like a lot of people blazed a trail for me. At some point I just started saying to myself, 'Why don't you set your own standards? Why don't you see how good you can be?' "

PRO FILE:

TIM
LINCEC

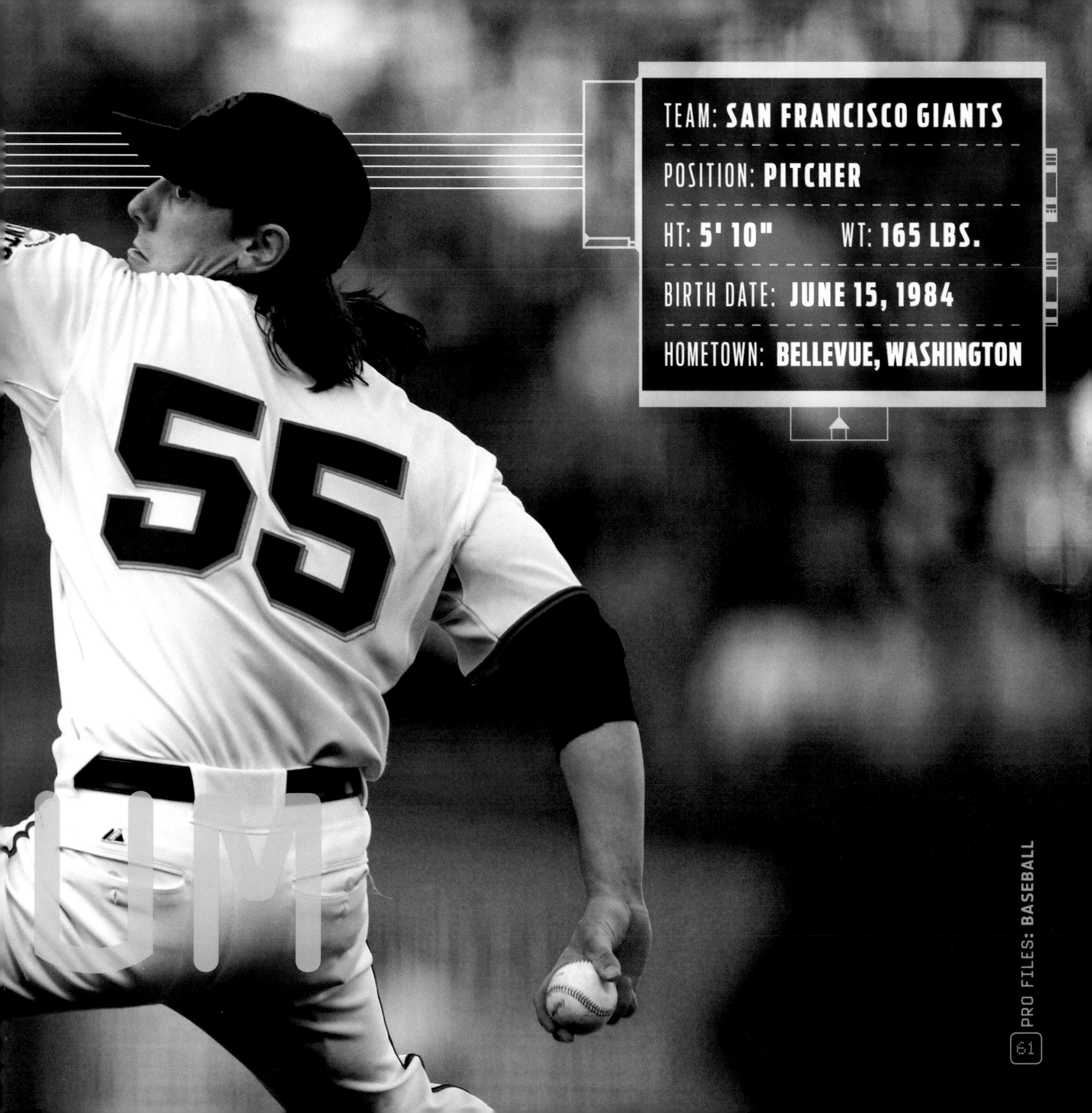

TEAM: **SAN FRANCISCO GIANTS**

POSITION: **PITCHER**

HT: **5' 10"**   WT: **165 LBS.**

BIRTH DATE: **JUNE 15, 1984**

HOMETOWN: **BELLEVUE, WASHINGTON**

TIM

BACKGROUND REPORT

>> At first glance, it's hard to believe that at 5' 10", 165 pounds, Tim Lincecum is a professional baseball player. Until you see him on the mound, that is. With terrific flexibility, deceiving strength, and a one-of-a-kind whirling windup that helps him throw a fastball in the mid-90s, Lincecum has been baffling big-league hitters over the past four seasons.

Growing up in Washington state, Lincecum was always small. But he was also uniquely flexible and athletic, allowing him to generate more velocity than bigger, stronger pitchers. His father, Chris, designed a special windup to get the most out of Lincecum's small frame. "My father pretty much taught me everything I know," Lincecum said. "He still pushes me to be the best I can."

It didn't make a huge difference early on. As a high school freshman, Lincecum was just 4' 11" and 85 pounds. He didn't make the varsity team until his junior year. But it proved to be worth the wait: He had a 0.73 ERA with 86 strikeouts in 49 innings as a junior. As a senior, everything fell into place. "I haven't always thrown hard," Lincecum said. "But eventually my [velocity] caught up with my mechanics."

In his final high school season, he could throw a 94-mile-per-hour fastball. He had a 0.70 ERA, struck out 183 in 91⅔ innings, and was named the state of Washington's Gatorade Player of the Year in 2003.

GIANT SUCCESS
A two-time NL Cy Young Award winner, Lincecum led San Francisco to the World Series title in 2010.

>>Small Wonder

The Chicago Cubs drafted Lincecum in the 48th round of the draft, but he opted for college at the nearby University of Washington. In his first season, he made history as the first player ever to be named both Pac-10 Freshman of the Year and Pitcher of the Year. After a dominant sophomore season, the Cleveland Indians drafted Lincecum in the 42nd round. But he decided to stay in college; he still had work to do for the Huskies. His junior year included school records for wins (12) and strikeouts (199). But because of his small frame, a lot of teams were nervous that Lincecum wouldn't be able to pitch every five days in the big leagues. Some saw him as a relief prospect. Others weren't convinced he'd make an impact in the majors at all. The San Francisco Giants took a chance on him, though, drafting Lincecum 10th overall in 2006.

If the Giants were just a little worried about Tiny Tim, it didn't last for long. Lincecum dominated the minor leagues over parts of two seasons (6–0, 1.01 ERA, 104 strikeouts in 62.2 innings). When he got to the big leagues in 2007, he struck out more than a batter per inning (150 in 146.1 innings). His breakthrough season came in 2008. Lincecum went 18–5 with a 2.62 ERA and a league-leading 265 strikeouts, winning the National League Cy Young Award. "In my 13 years in the big leagues, this is the only guy I've seen who is worth the hype," said teammate Rich Aurilia.

>>World Series Hero

A year later, Lincecum won the Cy Young again, going 15–7 with a 2.48 ERA and 261 strikeouts. "I never could have seen this happening growing up," he said. "You just try to put in the hard work and do the good things necessary to put yourself in this position."

He led the NL in strikcouts for a third straight season in 2010, and the Giants made the playoffs and the World Series for the first time in his career. Lincecum was asked to start Games 1 and 5 against the Texas Rangers. He delivered two wins. In Game 5, his 10 strikeouts over eight innings of one-run ball gave San Francisco its first World Series title.

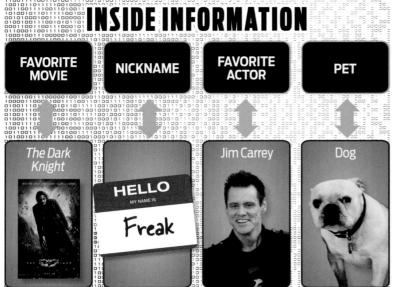

INSIDE INFORMATION

FAVORITE MOVIE	NICKNAME	FAVORITE ACTOR	PET
The Dark Knight	HELLO MY NAME IS Freak	Jim Carrey	Dog

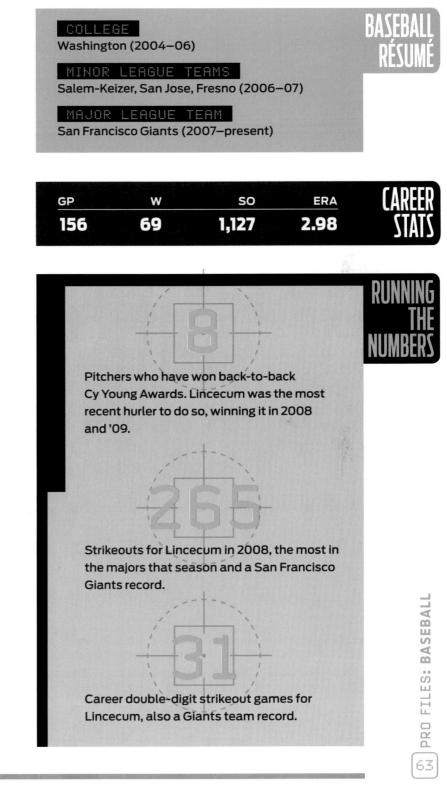

CAREER STATS

GP	W	SO	ERA
156	69	1,127	2.98

RUNNING THE NUMBERS

8
Pitchers who have won back-to-back Cy Young Awards. Lincecum was the most recent hurler to do so, winning it in 2008 and '09.

265
Strikeouts for Lincecum in 2008, the most in the majors that season and a San Francisco Giants record.

31
Career double-digit strikeout games for Lincecum, also a Giants team record.

SECRETS TO HIS GAME

Learn an Efficient Delivery Like Tim Lincecum

Lincecum is an out-of-this-world athlete because of his flexibility, coordination, and balance, which allow him to execute one of the most effective (and strangest) deliveries in baseball. Kids shouldn't mimic Lincecum's delivery — it is something that is special to him because of his abilities — but they may learn something from understanding how Lincecum's delivery works.

The key to his delivery is that Lincecum's body parts all work together. His flexibility and lower body strength are most apparent in his stride. (The normal stride length for a pitcher is 77 to 88 percent of his height. Lincecum's 7½-foot stride is 129 percent of his height.) "My dad always taught me to sit down on my back leg as long as I could and push off as much as I could," Lincecum said. "I've got to use my ankles, my legs, my hips, my back."

A long stride can be dangerous for a pitcher, but it works for Lincecum because his legs are strong enough to handle it. With his stride,

he releases the ball closer to home plate, meaning it will get there faster.

Once his left foot hits the ground, Lincecum is ready to finish off his delivery. His hips open so that his belt buckle is facing the plate. But, because of his flexibility, his

left shoulder is still pointing toward home. With his body twisted, he then unloads the pitch. His torso rotates and his arm follows with an over-the-top delivery. Or, as Lincecum puts it, "That's when everything kind of explodes. [My arm] is just along for the ride."

[+] Lincecum's unique delivery
[+] helps him generate power
[+] and arm speed with his
[+] small frame. But it also
[+] serves to confuse hitters
[+] who don't see that windup
[+] from anyone else. "He's a
[+] max-effort guy with a
[+] really different windup,"
[+] Chicago Cubs third
[+] baseman Ian Stewart told
[+] *Baseball America* after
[+] facing Lincecum in the
[+] minors. "You can't see the
[+] ball at all until it's right on
[+] top of you."
[+]   As if adjusting to his
[+] windup isn't tough enough,
[+] there are the pitches that
[+] come out of Lincecum's
[+] hand. While his fastball has
[+] lost some velocity since
[+] coming to the majors, he
[+] can still throw it in the
[+] mid-90s. He has
[+] always had a
[+] sharp-breaking
[+] curveball that
[+] comes in at
[+] 80 miles
[+] per hour.
[+] "When he
[+] was just

fastball–breaking ball, we'd
think, 'How is anybody
going to hit that?'"
teammate Matt Cain told
SPORTS ILLUSTRATED after
watching Lincecum as a
rookie. "Now you watch him
throw that split–change-up
thing, and it's unfair." The
"split-change-up thing"
Cain is referring to is the
change-up Lincecum uses
as his strikeout pitch. He
uses a split-finger grip. It
looks like his fastball, but
comes in 10 miles per hour
slower and dives down. He
can also make it move left
or right by adjusting the
finger pressure on the ball.
So even if hitters can detect
it's the change-up,
they don't
know
whether it
will move in at
their hands or
away from
them. It has
become
arguably the
best pitch in
baseball.

KNOW THE DRILL

Not surprisingly, some of Lincecum's
most important workouts involve his
legs and his core muscles: abdomen,
back, hips, and backside. He also
goes through a stretching routine
every day.

   Lincecum's father, Chris, came
up with a drill to stress the
importance of the follow-through
in Lincecum's delivery. He would put
a dollar on the ground in front of the
landing spot of Tim's left foot.
Tim would then have to pick up the
dollar on his follow-through after
releasing the ball.

   "My dad was always
stressing it," Lincecum
said. " 'Pick up the dollar!
If I put down a hundred-
dollar bill, you'd pick it up
every time!'"

IN HIS WORDS

" If I would've
listened to
all the people who
said I was too small,
I probably wouldn't
be here."

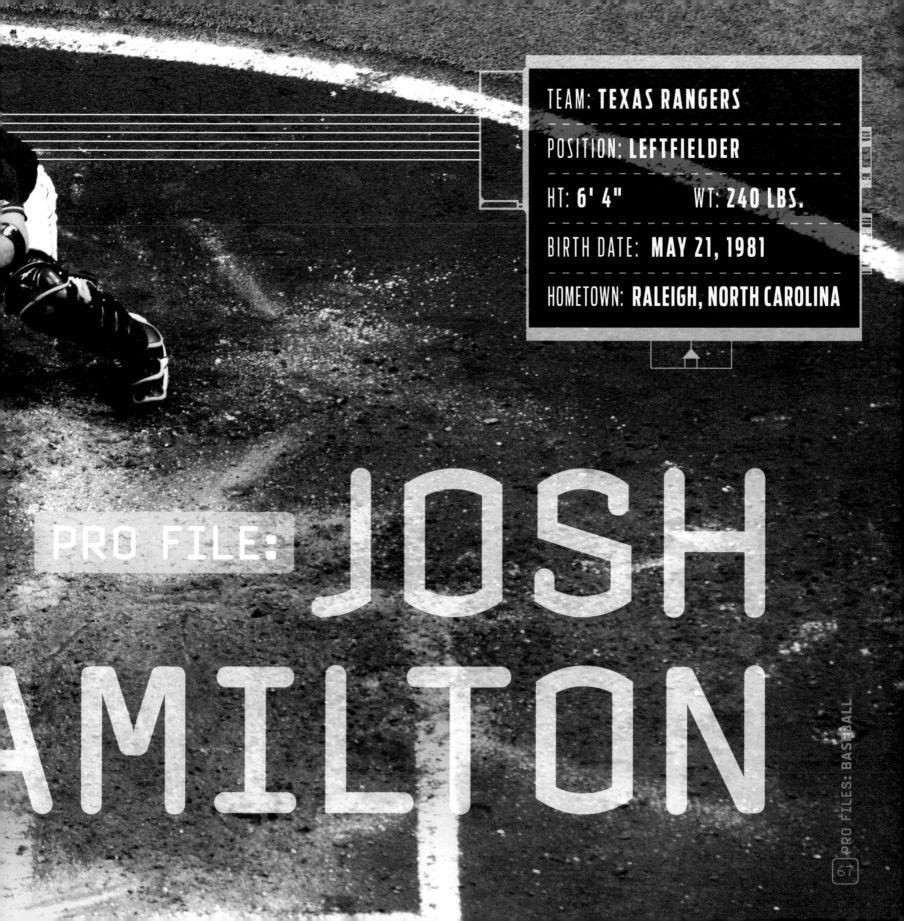

TEAM: **TEXAS RANGERS**

POSITION: **LEFTFIELDER**

HT: **6' 4"**   WT: **240 LBS.**

BIRTH DATE: **MAY 21, 1981**

HOMETOWN: **RALEIGH, NORTH CAROLINA**

PRO FILE: JOSH HAMILTON

JOSH HAMILTON

SMASH HIT
Hamilton was named the 2010 American League MVP after leading the league in batting (.359) and slugging (.633).

>> Josh Hamilton always seemed destined for greatness. He wasn't just another top prospect out of Athens Drive High School in Raleigh, North Carolina. He was a once-in-a-generation talent, with a dazzling left arm (as a pitcher in high school he consistently hit 96 miles per hour on the radar gun) and a vicious home-run swing (his bat speed was once clocked at an otherworldly 110 miles per hour). Hamilton was drafted Number 1 out of high school in the 1999 amateur draft by the Tampa Bay Devil Rays, which awarded him a then-record $3.96 million signing bonus.

"I remember seeing him taking batting practice with the Devil Rays in 2000 during spring training, and I was like, 'Who's that?'" says former major league first baseman Sean Casey. "He was 18 years old and hitting balls farther than anyone else. I went up and introduced myself, and I said, 'That's one of the greatest swings I've ever seen.' I don't think I've ever done that my whole career."

>>Fighting Back

But things didn't go as planned for the sweet-swinging Hamilton. The clean-cut, churchgoing boy who kissed his grandmother Mary before every one of his high school games got mixed up with the wrong crowd in the spring of 2001, after he suffered a back injury in a car accident and suddenly found himself with a lot of free time away from the baseball field. After struggling with drugs and alcohol, Hamilton was suspended from baseball in 2004 and didn't return until the Cincinnati Reds snagged him from the Rays in the Rule 5 draft in 2006. When he made his long-awaited major league debut on Opening Day 2007, he received a 22-second standing ovation as he stepped up to the plate for the first time in Cincinnati. He landed with the Rangers a year later, after being traded to Texas for pitcher Edinson Volquez. "Texas had faith in me," says Hamilton. "I couldn't have asked to have landed in a better situation, with teammates that embraced me with open arms."

With the Rangers, Hamilton finally began truly fulfilling his promise. In 2008, he was voted by fans to his first All-Star Game and put on a dazzling show in the Home Run Derby at Yankee Stadium, hitting three home runs that soared farther than 500 feet. In 2010, he won the American League batting title and the Most Valuable Player award. "He's really all everyone said he was," says Boston Red Sox pitcher Jon Lester. "He's strong, he's fast, he can hit, he can run. He's got real strong hands. It looks like he doesn't swing at a ball. He just flicks his wrist at it and the ball goes forever."

>>Shining in the Lone Star State

Hamilton is a big reason why the Rangers, historically among baseball's worst franchises, has become one of the giants of the

major leagues. During the 2010 American League Championship Series, he hit four home runs (even though Hamilton was intentionally walked five times in six games) and led Texas to its first-ever World Series appearance. In 2011, the Rangers won the AL West and returned to the Fall Classic for the second consecutive year, thanks to another All-Star season from the player who has battled back from as much adversity as any player in the majors. "Sometimes I step back and look at how far I've come, and even I can't believe it," says Hamilton. "It's been an incredible journey."

BASEBALL RÉSUMÉ

HIGH SCHOOL
Athens Drive

MINOR LEAGUE TEAMS
Princeton, Hudson Valley, Charleston, Orlando, Bakersfield, Louisville (1999–2007)

MAJOR LEAGUE TEAMS
Cincinnati Reds (2007), Texas Rangers (2008–present)

CAREER STATS

GP	AVG	HR	RBI
589	.308	118	425

RUNNING THE NUMBERS

490

Distance, in feet, of a home run Hamilton hit on June 27, 2010, at Rangers Ballpark in Arlington off the Phillies' Roy Oswalt. The home run, which landed in the seats in right centerfield, was the longest ever hit at the ballpark.

130

Runs batted in by Hamilton in 2008, his first full season in the majors. Hamilton's total was the highest in the American League that season.

28

Home runs Hamilton hit in the first round of the 2008 All-Star Home Run Derby at Yankee Stadium, the most ever in a single round of the derby. During one stretch Hamilton hit homers on 13 consecutive swings.

INSIDE INFORMATION

ATHLETE ADMIRED AS A KID	SHOE SIZE	FAVORITE CEREAL	NICKNAME
Tony Gwynn	19	Fruity Pebbles	Hambone

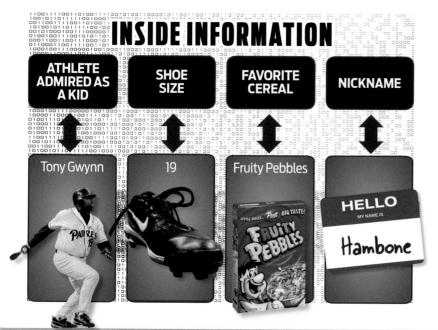

SECRETS TO HIS GAME

Take Pride in Playing Defense Like Josh Hamilton

Hamilton is one of today's biggest stars because he doesn't focus only on putting up big offensive numbers. "I realize that if I go 0 for 4 there are still other ways I can help us win," he says. "I can influence the outcome with my bat, but also my glove. I can't make an impact every night at the plate, but I can in the field." Hamilton isn't lightning quick, but he covers as much ground as any outfielder in the game. "He reacts to the ball off the bat as well as anyone," says Rangers manager Ron Washington. "He has great instincts." During batting practice, Hamilton stands in the outfield and works on reading balls off the bat and making throws into the infield. "I practice a lot in the outfield, with the other outfielders, as much as I do in the batting cages," says Hamilton. "It's fun for me. During a game, I'd rather throw a guy out than hit a home run."

IN HIS WORDS

"Playing all out and aggressive and leaving everything on the field is the only way I know how to play. If my career gets shortened by injuries from playing hard, or I didn't get 10 years in because I played [too] hard, then that's the way it's going to be."

INSIDE HIS SWING

Hamilton used to take a step forward with his front foot when he swung at a ball, but he had trouble connecting with off-speed pitches on the outside part of the plate. So he started using a toe-tap technique. When he begins to swing, he brings his front foot back a few inches, taps the tip of the shoe on the ground, and then puts the front foot back to its original position. "It helps me stay balanced and stay back on off-speed pitches and breaking balls," he says, "and allows me to get to pitches on the outside of the plate and put good wood on the ball."

PLAYER ANALYSIS

[+] Hamilton is one of the most
[+] complete baseball players in
[+] the majors. He is most known
[+] for his legendary home-run
[+] power — "He puts on shows
[+] during batting practice; it's
[+] hard not to just sit back and
[+] watch the bombs he hits,"
[+] says Rangers second
[+] baseman Ian Kinsler — but he
[+] also has one of the best
[+] defensive gloves in the
[+] outfield. Ask Texas general
[+] manager Jon Daniels for a
[+] memorable Josh Hamilton
[+] moment from recent years,
[+] and he names three defensive
[+] plays, all of which preserved
[+] wins for the Rangers.

[+] Says Phillies outfielder Raul
[+] Ibañez, "[Hamilton] plays the
[+] shallowest [outfield] I've ever
[+] seen, and he can still go and
[+] get the ball like nobody's
[+] business."
[+]   "Watching him play is
[+] exciting," says former A's
[+] pitcher Greg Smith. "The ball
[+] just sounds different coming
[+] off his bat, almost like a
[+] gunshot. You watch him
[+] track down a ball, you watch
[+] him throw a guy out at third
[+] base. Then he hits a ball
[+] down the line and gets a
[+] triple and it's like, 'The guy
[+] can run too? You've gotta be
[+] kidding me.'"

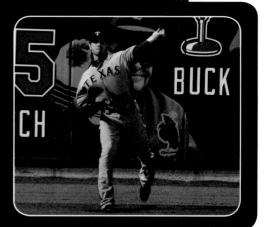

PRO FILE:

JOSE R

TEAM: **MIAMI MARLINS**

POSITION: **SHORTSTOP**

HT: **6' 1"**   WT: **200 LBS.**

BIRTH DATE: **JUNE 11, 1983**

HOMETOWN: **PALMAR ARRIBA, DOMINICAN REPUBLIC**

EYES

BACKGROUND REPORT

>>> There was nothing particularly special about Jose Reyes when he was a boy growing up in the village of Palmar Arriba in the Dominican Republic. He had legs like twigs and skinny arms, just like most of the other boys he played with on the neighborhood ball fields. Even as a teenager he wasn't particularly fast on the bases, nor did he have much of an arm. It was hard enough to believe that he would one day play outside of his home country, let alone make it to the major leagues and become one of the best players in the game.

But one afternoon when Reyes was 16, a scout from the New York Mets named Eddy Toledo stood on the field during a tryout camp in the town of Santiago, not far from Reyes's home. Toledo saw something special in the kid. "It was like he had a halo over his head," Toledo says. While scouts from other teams would not give the scrawny 6'0",

BIG HIT

Although he wasn't heavily scouted, Reyes established himself as one of the best players in the game.

160-pound Reyes even a second glance, Toledo was intrigued by the way he carried himself on the field: his confidence, his flair while making the most routine fielding play. After the tryout, Toledo invited Reyes's family for lunch and soon after signed him to a modest $13,000 bonus, which was not much compared with the millions given to first-round draft picks or well-regarded Dominican prospects. It proved to be money well spent.

>>Hometown Hero

In the Mets' minor league system, Reyes blossomed into one of the top prospects in baseball, a phenom whose debut in the majors became an eagerly awaited event both in New York and in the Dominican Republic. When a 19-year-old Reyes played in his first big-league game, in June 2003, his family in Palmar Arriba opened the doors of their house and played a broadcast of the game on the radio. The townspeople flooded the street as Reyes's smashing debut (he singled and doubled against the Texas Rangers) became a city-wide celebration deep into the night. The celebration has continued during Reyes's nine-season career. "I know every game that they

are watching back home," says Reyes. "It makes me very proud."

Reyes still has a childlike enthusiasm for the game, and his passion and talent quickly made him one of the most popular players in New York, where he was the engine for the Mets' offense and one of the most dynamic leadoff hitters in the game.

"He's the kind of guy that when he's at the plate when the TV is on, you stop and watch," says Dodgers general manager Ned Colletti. "He has that kind of talent and charisma."

>>Move to Miami

A new chapter in Reyes's career began in December 2011 when he accepted a six-year, $106 million contract with the Miami Marlins, a team that wants to make Reyes the new face of the franchise as it moves into a new ballpark. Though he's moving from the skyscrapers and pressures of the Big Apple to the sunshine of South Florida, Reyes remains as motivated as ever to prove that he's one of the best players in the game. "There are always ways to get better," he says. "I'm never going to stop trying to be as good as I can be."

HIGH SCHOOL
Santiago

MINOR LEAGUE TEAMS
Kingsport, Columbia, St. Lucie, Binghamton, Norfolk (2000–03)

MAJOR LEAGUE TEAMS
New York Mets (2003–2011), Florida Marlins (present)

CAREER STATS

GP	AVG.	HR	RBI
1,050	.292	81	423

RUNNING THE NUMBERS

4

Seasons Reyes has led the National League in triples since 2003. He is the Mets' all-time triples leader (99).

370

Career stolen bases by Reyes. He led the majors in that category in 2005, '06, and '07.

.337

Batting average for Reyes in 2011, the highest in the NL. Reyes became the first Mets player to win a batting title.

INSIDE INFORMATION

FIRST CAR	NICKNAME	FAVORITE FOOD	ATHLETE ADMIRED AS A KID
Mitsubishi	La Melaza (sweetness in Spanish)	Fried chicken and beans	Juan Marichal

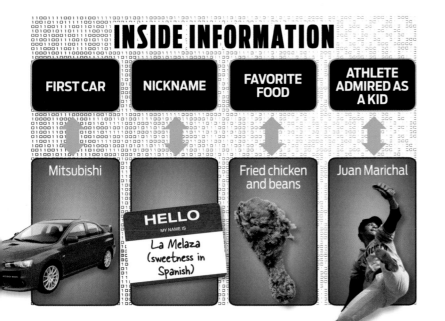

SECRETS TO HIS GAME

Run the Bases Like Jose Reyes

What's the key to being a good base runner? "Run hard right out of the box and don't hesitate at all," says Reyes. "When you're running, if you don't think you're going to make it [safely], you're probably not going to make it. For me, 99.9 percent of the time, I *know* I'm going to make it."

Reyes attributes his success as a base stealer to Hall of Famer Rickey Henderson, whom former Mets general manager Omar Minaya brought in to school the shortstop early in his career. Henderson taught Reyes to read pitches in the dirt. "If you're on first, you should go if you know the ball is going to bounce," says Reyes. "If you see the catcher block the ball, it's too late."

When he's on second base, Reyes knows to go for third if the ball gets away from the catcher. By being an aggressive base runner, you "distract the pitcher," says Reyes. "You become a headache for the other team."

PRE-GAME ROUTINE

When Reyes first started playing in the majors, he was so young and talented that he could get by without pushing himself. But after battling several injuries, Reyes has learned the value of preparation and hard work away from the ballpark. "When you're young, you just run out to the field and not worry about anything," says Reyes. "Now I know my body better [and] what I have to do better. I never had a routine before. Now I do."

Before Reyes goes to the stadium, he gets a massage to loosen his muscles. When he gets to the ballpark at 2:15 p.m. for night games, he sits in a tub of hot water. Then he stretches before hitting the batting cages and stretches again before batting practice. About a half hour before first pitch, he hits the batting cage for more drills. "I'm not as fast as I was when I was younger," he says, "but I feel as healthy and strong as ever."

PLAYER ANALYSIS

[+] Reyes is a natural righthander
[+] who began swinging from the
[+] left side only a few months
[+] before he was signed by the
[+] Mets in 1999. Now he's one of
[+] the best switch-hitters in the
[+] game. (A .302 career hitter
[+] from the right side, he hits
[+] .288 as a lefty.) Scouts once
[+] called him a player with
[+] 25-home-run potential, but
[+] Reyes, who has never hit more
[+] than 19 home runs in a season,
[+] is more of a doubles and
[+] triples hitter. "He's got a level
[+] swing, and he's great at
[+] making a lot of good contact,"

[+] says Mets G.M. Sandy
[+] Alderson. "He's a premier gap
[+] hitter, which with his speed is a
[+] good combination."
[+]   But Reyes's greatness does
[+] not end with his bat. "He can
[+] impact a game with his bat,
[+] his glove, and his speed," says
[+] Mets third baseman David
[+] Wright. "There aren't too
[+] many players with his
[+] combination of weapons."
[+] The only thing that's held
[+] Reyes back are injuries. Says
[+] Wright, "When he's healthy,
[+] there isn't a more dynamic
[+] player in baseball."

HEI

TEAM: **SEATTLE MARINERS**

POSITION: **PITCHER**

HT: **6' 3"**   WT: **225 LBS.**

BIRTH DATE: **APRIL 8, 1986**

HOMETOWN: **VALENCIA, VENEZUELA**

RO FILE: FELIX

.NANDEZ

FELIX HERNANDEZ

BACKGROUND REPORT

>> Felix Hernandez was only 17 years old when he became king. At the time, he was mowing down batters in the minor leagues. He had such amazing stuff and was so dominant that Seattle Mariners fans were already getting excited about their top prospect. A popular Mariners blogger gave him a hopeful nickname: King Felix. Eight years later, it's clear that the crown fits.

Mariners scouts first spotted Hernandez when he was 14 and throwing a 90 mile-per-hour fastball. But, under MLB rules, the hard-throwing righty couldn't be signed until he turned 16.

"The first time I saw him, I knew he was something special," Mariners scout Emilio Carrasquel told the *Seattle Post-Intelligencer.*

The waiting was painful. Other teams started to take notice of Hernandez. The Atlanta Braves offered him a lot of money. The New York Yankees offered him a contract too. But Hernandez and his family were most comfortable with Seattle. It didn't hurt that the Mariners' ace at the time was Freddy Garcia, a Venezuelan pitcher who was Hernandez's idol.

WORTH THE WAIT
The Mariners discovered Hernandez when he was 14 years old — 10 years later he was the AL Cy Young Award winner.

>>Young Gun

From 2003 through '05, Hernandez dominated in the minors. Along with an electric fastball, Hernandez had a devastating curve and, unlike many young pitchers, a great feel for his change-up. Even as a teenager, he appeared destined for greatness. *Baseball America* wrote, in a 2004 scouting report of Hernandez, "Arm problems would appear to be the only thing that could derail him from stardom."

Because of the risk of injury, Seattle took it slow with its prized prospect. Midway through the 2005 season, Hernandez had struck out 100 batters in 88 innings as one of the youngest players in Triple A. The Mariners knew he was far too good for the minors, so on August 4, 2005, Hernandez made his big-league debut at the age of 19. He was the youngest pitcher in the majors in 21 years.

Hernandez held the Detroit Tigers to one earned run over five innings, but he still took a tough-luck loss. Things would get a lot better very quickly. In his second start, Hernandez threw eight shutout innings in a victory over the Minnesota Twins. And six days later, he struck out 11 over eight innings in a win over the Kansas City Royals. Hernandez made 12 starts in his rookie year, finishing with 77 strikeouts in 84⅓ innings and a 2.67 ERA, third best among American League pitchers who made at least 10 starts.

"I remember facing him in 2005," said shortstop Jack Wilson, who would later become a teammate of Hernandez. "Felix was a young kid with an incredible arm who threw hard and had a great off-speed pitch."

>>Strikeout King

Coming off his strong rookie season, Hernandez may have taken it too easy over the winter, showing up out of shape for spring training in

2006. It showed in his performance that season. His ERA was as high as 5.10 at one point in late June, and he finished the year with a 12–14 record and a 4.52 ERA. Having learned his lesson about conditioning, Hernandez began to take his off-season training seriously. In 2007, he began his rise to baseball's elite.

His ERA improved every season from 2007 through 2010, when he had an MLB-best 2.27 mark to go along with a career-high 232 strikeouts. Although poor run support led to only 13 wins in 2010, Hernandez became the first starting pitcher to win a Cy Young Award with fewer than 15 victories in a non-strike year.

"This is the first of many," Hernandez said after he received the award. "Now I have to work even harder, because I'm the best pitcher in the American League."

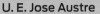

HIGH SCHOOL
U. E. Jose Austre

MINOR LEAGUE TEAMS
Everett, Wisconsin, Inland Empire, San Antonio, Tacoma (2003–05)

MAJOR LEAGUE TEAM
Seattle Mariners (2005–present)

CAREER STATS

GP	W	SO	ERA
205	85	1,264	3.24

RUNNING THE NUMBERS

24
Hernandez's age (in years, plus 139 days) when he recorded his 1,000th career strikeout, on August 25, 2010. He became the fourth-youngest pitcher in MLB history to reach 1,000 strikeouts.

13
Wins by Hernandez in 2010. It was the fewest wins ever for a Cy Young Award–winning starting pitcher in a non-strike season. He received little run support that season (3.77 runs per game) but had a 2.27 ERA and 232 strikeouts.

2.72
ERA for Hernandez from 2009 through '11, the lowest among American League starters during that span.

INSIDE INFORMATION

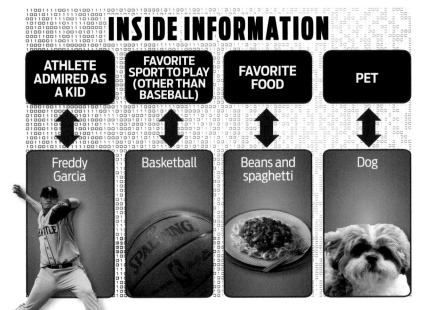

ATHLETE ADMIRED AS A KID	FAVORITE SPORT TO PLAY (OTHER THAN BASEBALL)	FAVORITE FOOD	PET
Freddy Garcia	Basketball	Beans and spaghetti	Dog

SECRETS TO HIS GAME

Fool Hitters Like Felix Hernandez

Hernandez has one of the best change-ups in the game. "I think every young pitcher should learn a change-up before they learn a curveball," says Seattle Mariners pitching coach Carl Willis. "It's a 'feel' pitch, and it can be tough to get that feel down late in your career."

In the youngest baseball leagues, throwing a slightly slower pitch might be beneficial for the batter. But when you get to higher levels of competition, such as high school, hitters will catch up to your fastball. An effective change-up will throw off a batter's timing for an entire at-bat. The circle change, the most basic form of the pitch, can be very effective. Instead of your regular grip, move the ball toward the pinky finger side of your hand. Your index finger should be on the side of the ball, and your index finger and thumb form the circle. "Really focus on throwing the pitch with the same arm speed and the same arm slot," Willis says. "The grip is going to take the velocity off."

A change-up moves slower than the fastball, but not because your arm is moving slower. It's due to the fact that all five fingers are in contact with the ball, creating more friction, which slows down the pitch. The reason it's so deceptive is that when the batter sees your arm moving like it does on a fastball, he will probably expect a fastball and swing too early.

IN HIS WORDS

> " I know this game is physical, but the mental part is so important."

THE CIRCLE CHANGE

Don't run onto the mound and start trying to throw a change-up immediately. Willis recommends getting used to your grip by simply using it in a game of catch. "Start off throwing it on flat ground," Willis says. "Get used to the grip during warmup or a game of catch."

Once you're able to throw your fastball with two fingers (as opposed to younger Little Leaguers, who sometimes have to use three fingers or their whole hand to grip the ball), the best way to learn a change-up is to move the ball back in your hand and put your ring finger on top of it. That will create more friction and more resistance on the ball coming out of your hand.

As you get comfortable with the grip, you can start to move the ball out toward your pinky, placing both your middle and ring fingers on top of the ball. Bend your index finger as shown in the photo, and that's the circle change. "Some guys hold it right in the center, and some guys hold it a little off to the side," says Willis. "It's all individualized feel."

PLANER ANALYSIS

[+] Like with any dominant
[+] pitcher, Felix Hernandez's
[+] success starts with his
[+] fastball. Or, in Hernandez's
[+] case, fastballs.
[+] "He throws two fastballs,
[+] a four-seamer and a two-
[+] seamer," says an American
[+] League scout for an
[+] opposing team. "His four-
[+] seamer has a little more
[ ] velocity to it, and he can
throw it on the plate or off
the plate.
"His two-seamer is
almost like a heavy sinker.
It looks like a four-seamer
and then — boom! — it
dives down at your feet."

[+] Hernandez has come a
[+] long way from the days of
[+] being a hard-throwing
[+] teenager. These days,
[+] Hernandez's secondary
[+] pitches are just as good
[+] as his heat.
[+] "He didn't have his huge
[+] fastball [in 2011]," says the
[+] scout. "But he threw a bunch
[+] of really good change-ups,
[+] sliders, and curveballs. He
[+] can do that. All his pitches
[+] are deceptive, and he can
[+] get the big strikeout when
[+] he needs it. He's got a
[+] dominating change-up. It
[+] just disappears."
[+] The best might be yet to

[+] come for the ace.
[+] The scout sees
[+] Hernandez as a
[+] pitcher capable
[+] of winning
[+] 25 games.
[+] "What
[+] makes him
[+] really unique,"
[+] the scout says,
[+] "is that he
[+] needs hardly
[+] any help from
[+] the offense, and
[+] he can still win
[+] 80 percent of his
[+] starts. That's
[+] rare to see
[+] these days."

PRO FILE:

BRIAN

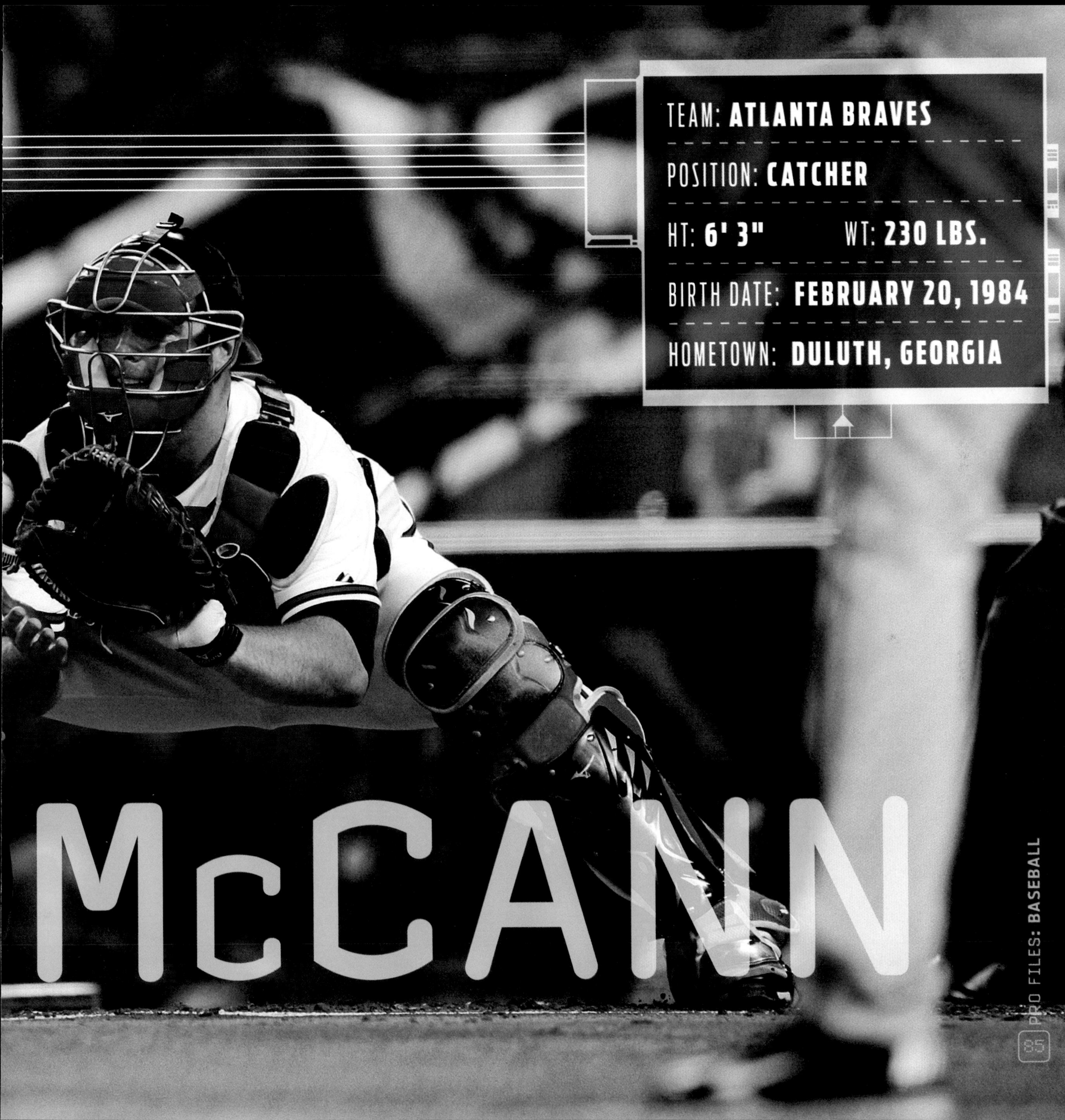

TEAM: **ATLANTA BRAVES**

POSITION: **CATCHER**

HT: **6' 3"**   WT: **230 LBS.**

BIRTH DATE: **FEBRUARY 20, 1984**

HOMETOWN: **DULUTH, GEORGIA**

McCANN

BACKGROUND REPORT

>> Baseball runs in Brian McCann's blood. His brother, Brad, who is 14 months older, always played growing up, and his father, Howie, was an assistant baseball coach at the University of Georgia and a head coach at Marshall University in West Virginia. It was as a kid in West Virginia that McCann first learned to swing for average and power. Long before he became a six-time All-Star catcher with the Atlanta Braves — and the youngest catcher to homer in a playoff game, when he hit one off Roger Clemens as a 21-year-old rookie in 2005 — McCann hit his first monumental home run as a 10-year-old competing for a regional championship in West Virginia. His father had overheard parents of the opposing team say to one another, "We can't let this kid beat us tonight." Yet McCann still delivered, crushing a walk-off home run in the sixth inning to win the title.

>>Perennial All-Star

The McCanns returned to Georgia in 1996, when Brian was 12. His hometown Atlanta Braves had just won the World Series and were in the early stages of

SWEET SWING
A five-time Silver Slugger award winner, McCann led NL catchers in home runs (24) and ranked second in RBIs (71) in 2011.

what would become a 14-year streak of winning divisional titles. McCann became friends with another local youth player, Jeff Francoeur, and they starred together on travel teams. McCann also played at Duluth (Georgia) High alongside his brother, Brad. Brad went on to excel at Clemson and play minor league ball for the Florida Marlins and the Kansas City Royals, while Brian was selected in the second round of the 2002 draft by the Braves.

McCann homered in his second major league game, as a 21-year-old in June 2005. In 2006, he became Atlanta's starting catcher, joining the same lineup as his childhood friend Francoeur, who started in rightfield. McCann batted .333 that year with 24 home runs and 93 RBIs and made the first of six consecutive All-Star teams. "Being selected as an All-Star is such a huge honor, and it hits you when you walk in that locker room," McCann says. "You see the best players in the game, and you're sitting around and you've got to pinch yourself sometimes that you're able to share this locker room and share this field."

McCann is being modest — he belongs on the list as one of the brightest stars in the game. A consistent offensive threat among catchers, McCann leads all major league backstops over the last six seasons in home runs (131) and is second in doubles (193) and RBIs (514). "He puts everything he has into each at-bat, into calling a game, into throwing runners out," Braves catcher David Ross told *The Atlanta Journal-Constitution*. "He wants to be the perfect player."

INSIDE INFORMATION

FAVORITE ACTRESS	FAVORITE TEAM AS A KID	PRE-GAME MUSIC	HOBBY
Jessica Biel	Atlanta Braves	Jason Aldean	Playing Xbox

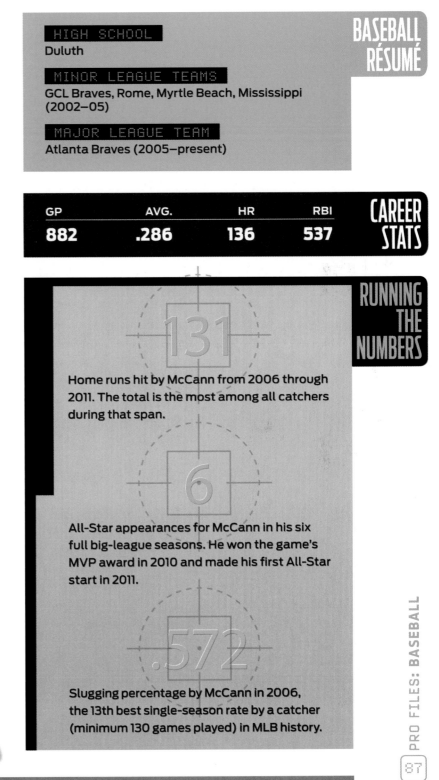

BASEBALL RÉSUMÉ

HIGH SCHOOL
Duluth

MINOR LEAGUE TEAMS
GCL Braves, Rome, Myrtle Beach, Mississippi (2002–05)

MAJOR LEAGUE TEAM
Atlanta Braves (2005–present)

CAREER STATS

GP	AVG.	HR	RBI
882	.286	136	537

RUNNING THE NUMBERS

131
Home runs hit by McCann from 2006 through 2011. The total is the most among all catchers during that span.

6
All-Star appearances for McCann in his six full big-league seasons. He won the game's MVP award in 2010 and made his first All-Star start in 2011.

.572
Slugging percentage by McCann in 2006, the 13th best single-season rate by a catcher (minimum 130 games played) in MLB history.

SECRETS TO HIS GAME

Hit Line Drives Like Brian McCann

"The key to hitting," says Brian's father, Howie McCann, "is hitting line drives." The best way to do that is to have a nice level swing. Some young players struggle in visualizing how that looks after starting with their hands held high, so Howie, a former head coach at Marshall University and a current instructor at the Windward Baseball Academy, teaches hitters to make the same swing path with their bat as an airplane does to land. "[My father] uses a lot of analogies, but that was one that stuck with me," Brian says. "That's the path you have to take to hit a baseball."

[1]

Your hands should hold the bat high, at about the same level as your ear. As the ball is pitched, shift your weight back and start swinging the bat at a 45-degree angle downward toward the plate.

[2]

Aim to make contact with the baseball when it's about six inches in front of the plate. Start to level your swing so that you "square up the baseball" — which means to hit the middle of the ball with the bat. "The plane comes in at 45 degrees and levels off," Howie says.

[3]

Fully extending your arms is an important part of the swing. Continue swinging through the ball just as a plane would "go down the runway to the terminal," Howie says.

ALL IN THE FAMILY

McCann's talent and work ethic have led to his major league success, but the fact that he has such a supportive family with a deep knowledge of the game has also helped the catcher a lot along the way.

Early in 2011, when he was hitting for a high average but not much power, his brother, Brad, gave him a few tips over the phone — and Brian homered twice the next day. Brian also seeks the advice of his father, who taught him his swing. "What's fun for me is when people say, 'Your kid has got such an easy, simple swing,'" Howie McCann says.

IN HIS WORDS

" Being a catcher, it's like a fraternity because it is such a demanding position, mentally and physically. I take a lot of pride in showing up and trying to play as many games as I can."

PLAYER ANALYSIS

[+] While many clubs
[+] sacrifice offense
[+] to find a good
[+] defensive catcher,
[+] McCann is a bonus
[+] for the Braves. He
[+] hits for the right
[+] combination of
[+] average and
[+] power to make
[+] him a key contributor in the middle
[+] of Atlanta's lineup, winning five
[+] Silver Slugger awards as the NL's
[+] best offensive catcher. In those five
[+] years he batted .290 while slugging
[+] .499 and averaging 23 homers per
[+] season. In fact, he has started only
[+] four games batting somewhere
[+] other than third, fourth, or fifth
[+] in the lineup during the last
[+] three seasons.
[+] Like most lefthanded batters,
[+] McCann hits righties better
[+] (.295 for his career, with a home
[+] run every 21 at-bats), but he hits
[+] lefties reasonably well too (.266
[+] with a homer every 27 at-bats).
[+] McCann may not win a Gold Glove
[+] for his defense, but he's a sturdy
[+] receiver behind the plate who has
[+] caught legends such as John
[+] Smoltz and Tom Glavine and
[+] All-Stars such as Tim Hudson,
[+] Jonny Venters, and Craig Kimbrel.

TEAM: **NEW YORK YANKEES**

POSITION: **PITCHER**

HT: **6' 2"**   WT: **185 LBS.**

BIRTH DATE: **NOVEMBER 29, 1969**

HOMETOWN: **PANAMA CITY, PANAMA**

MARIANO RIVERA

BACKGROUND REPORT

>> The bullpen door swings open, and Mariano Rivera begins his jog to the mound as his signature entrance music, Metallica's "Enter Sandman," blares on the speakers. The moment is ominous for teams visiting Yankee Stadium — they know that when New York's closer comes into a game with a lead in the ninth inning, there's a slim chance that they'll rally for a win. No reliever in baseball history has been as dominant as Rivera, whose job for the Yankees is to finish teams off by notching the last few outs of the game. "Being a closer is probably the most pressure-filled job in baseball," says Rivera's longtime catcher Jorge Posada. "But Mo makes it look like a piece of cake."

Of the Yankees' famous Core Four — Rivera, Posada, shortstop Derek Jeter, and former starter Andy Pettitte, who have anchored the Yankees during their stretch of excellence going back to the late 1990s — you could make the argument that no player has been more valuable than Number 42. Rivera's greatness has been a constant in the Bronx, and few players in baseball history have been as clutch in the postseason as the pitcher who got the final outs of the Yankees' last four World Series wins (1998, '99, 2000, '09). "We don't get to the playoffs, we don't win the championships, we don't do all the things we were able to do all those years without this guy," says Posada.

CASE CLOSED
Having already won five World Series titles, Rivera added another accomplishment to his Hall of Fame career when he surpassed Trevor Hoffman as the all-time saves leader in 2011.

>>Discovering His Cutter

The son of a fisherman, Rivera grew up in a tiny Panamanian village, where he played baseball on beaches and streets using sticks as bats and milk cartons as gloves. In 1990, he was discovered by a Yankees scout, who signed the little-known prospect to a relatively small $3,500 bonus.

It didn't take long for Rivera to make an impact: In his first full season with the Yankees, in 1996, he struck out 130 batters in 107⅔ innings as a middle reliever. But it wasn't until the summer of 1997, the year he was promoted to the role of closer, that Rivera, by accident, discovered the pitch that would make him an all-time great. He had been fiddling with the grip on his four-seam fastball, but one afternoon during his daily toss with his teammate Ramiro Mendoza, Rivera noticed that his fastball suddenly had wicked movement on it. He started throwing it in games, and ever since he's used that pitch — known as the cut fastball — as his primary weapon against hitters.

"It was a gift from God," he says of his cut fastball. "One day I was just able to throw it. I'm blessed that it's worked for me as long as it has."

>>In the Record Books

On the afternoon of September 19, 2011, Rivera entered the ninth inning of a game against the Minnesota Twins at Yankee Stadium. He pitched a perfect 1-2-3 inning to preserve a 6–4 win for New York, but more notably, he got his 602nd career save, which allowed him to pass Trevor Hoffman as baseball's all-time saves leader.

At age 41 and in his 17th season, Rivera showed no signs of slowing down as he completed his eighth season with 40 or more saves. "All closers look up to him," says Texas Rangers closer Joe Nathan. "He's the best that there's ever been and ever will be. There's just never going to be another Mariano Rivera."

INSIDE INFORMATION

FAVORITE TEAM TO WATCH	FAVORITE MOVIE	FAVORITE FOOD	FAVORITE TV SHOW
Brazilian men's national soccer team	The Rock	Italian	SportsCenter

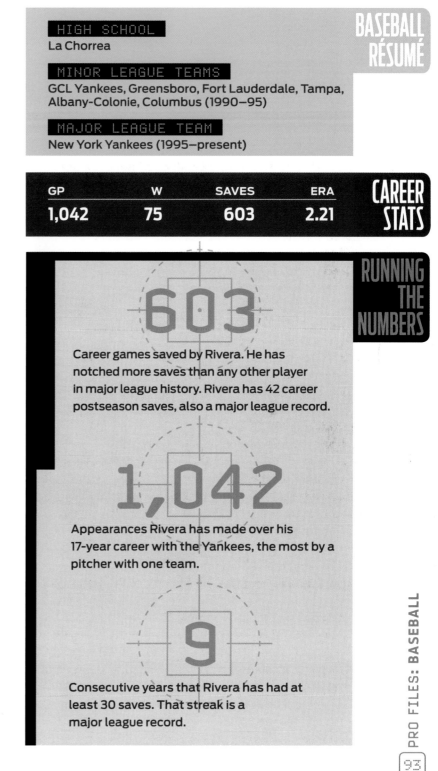

CAREER STATS

GP	W	SAVES	ERA
1,042	75	603	2.21

RUNNING THE NUMBERS

603

Career games saved by Rivera. He has notched more saves than any other player in major league history. Rivera has 42 career postseason saves, also a major league record.

1,042

Appearances Rivera has made over his 17-year career with the Yankees, the most by a pitcher with one team.

9

Consecutive years that Rivera has had at least 30 saves. That streak is a major league record.

SECRETS TO HIS GAME

Be Mentally Tough Like Mariano Rivera

Closers have to be particularly mentally strong because of the nature of their job. "If you blow a save, you have to be able to come right back the next day in another high-pressure situation," says closer Joe Nathan. "When it's your job to come into a game with a slim lead in the final inning night after night, it can be really taxing mentally."

It's a testament to Rivera's toughness and determination that he's been able to sustain his excellence for nearly two decades. No one has proven to be better at focusing during clutch situations. Rivera's key is his ability to block out everything except the task at hand. "Sometimes I see only the catcher's glove," Rivera says. "Sometimes there is nothing else, not even the hitter. You have to have that kind of focus."

Rivera's expression rarely changes, even if he gives up a home run. He sees his low-key demeanor as a weapon. "You can't let the other team know that you're shaken up, even if you are," says Rivera. "You can't let them get to you. You have to be the same day after day, pitch after pitch, no matter what."

SPECIAL DELIVERY

As a pitcher who has relied on one pitch for virtually his entire Hall of Fame career, Rivera knows the importance of being able to repeat his delivery over and over. Rivera's delivery is remarkably efficient, allowing him to throw the ball with the same release point and the same arm angle. "His mechanics are so easy, so perfect, it's like he could pitch this way until he's past [age] 50," says Jorge Posada.

Rivera has been able to sustain his brilliance for so long because he's a natural athlete who is always committed to keeping his body in tip-top shape. "He looks exactly like the same pitcher he was when he was a young pitcher in the majors," says Cardinals outfielder Lance Berkman. "He's a machine."

PLAYER ANALYSIS

[+] Rivera has only one pitch, so
[+] the hitter at the plate knows
[+] exactly what's coming when
[+] Rivera is on the mound. Then
[+] why can't hitters catch up to
[+] Rivera's cut fastball? "He
[+] throws different versions of it
[+] to keep you on your toes,"
[+] says Berkman. Rivera can
[+] throw the classic cutter that
[+] cuts inside — into the hands
[+] of a lefty — or he can start

[+] the pitch off the plate and
[+] make it cut back to the
[+] outside corner, a variation of
[+] the pitch known as the
[+] backdoor cutter. By changing
[+] the amount of pressure he
[+] applies on the ball with his
[+] fingertips, he can vary how
[+] much the ball cuts.
[+]   "A hitter can't track a pitch
[+] all the way to the point of
[+] contact," says Berkman.

[+] "Your eyes can't keep their
[+] focus on something moving
[+] that fast toward you. What
[+] makes Mariano's cutter so
[+] tough is that you can't see
[+] the spin on it and track it —
[+] one moment the ball looks
[+] like it's right there, and you
[+] go to hit it, and the next
[+] thing you know it's right at
[+] your hands, and you look
[+] like a fool."

IN HIS WORDS

" **My mental approach is simple: Get three outs as quick as possible. If I can throw three, four pitches, the better it is. I don't care how I get you out, as long as I get you out. That's the only thing I have in mind."**